Basic Windcraft
Using The Wind For Sailing

Alan Watts

Illustrated by Mary Sims

Dodd, Mead & Company
New York

Acknowledgements
My rough drawings have been turned into finished artwork by Mary Sims of Portman Artists. Real boats have been combined with real skies so that the backgrounds illustrate the weather that goes with the points being made.
PAGE 57
(More detailed notes on these winds can be found in 'Sailing on Continental Lakes' J. B. Moore)

By the same author
Wind and Sailing Boats   David and Charles
Instant Weather Forecasting   Dodd, Mead
Instant Wind Forecasting   Dodd, Mead
Wind Pilot   Nautical Publishing Company

ISBN: 0-396-07326-3

Library of Congress Catalog Card Number 75-42832

Printed in Great Britain

Contents

About this Book

This is a book of pictures with extended captions which covers the elementary things that sailing people ought to know about their motive power — the wind.

It tends to complement similar books on the techniques of sailing and seamanship such as *Starting Sailing*, which is a companion to this volume. Compared to the many books that exist on the various skills required to helm a sailing boat it can be fairly safely said that this is the first book that has attempted to tell helmsmen and crews in picture form about this invisible entity they use to such great advantage.

If you met the invisible man it would be useful to know how he usually acted so that he did not have too great an advantage over you and also to help avoid dangerous and painful collisions with him. The wind is the same. It is an invisible man whose attributes and whereabouts are always directly veiled from us and only by observing other things can we see it moving here and ghosting there. Strangely enough we have grown entirely used to the invisibility of the wind. Nowhere in this book can there be a direct illustration of the wind. We draw arrows and mark directions and judge speed by the state of sea and the way the trees bend and how far out the dinghy crews are sitting. This is the way of our motive power and we do not find it at all surprising that we sail so accurately in a medium we have never directly seen.

One reason for this is that a sailing boat is a pretty good arrow for the wind. Once the boat is sailing and we have a masthead flag, or tell-tales in very light airs, then we tend to know where the wind is. Yet how much better if we can visualise a shift on the way from signs that exist but which are not universally obvious. That is where windcraft comes into its own. I have coined this term of windcraft from remembering that forest dwellers live in equilibrium with their, often hostile, environment by the use of forest-craft or woodcraft. The man knowledgeable in woodcraft devines things from small signs that the novice would never even notice.

So it is with the sailing science of windcraft. Those who are knowledge-able will see signs that others miss and so will make up a place or two here and another there as they pick their way through the shifts. And there are times when tactical situations are totally transformed by the correct use of an anticipated change of wind. The others will use the shift, but you use it first and to better advantage because you know it is coming. A top helmsman recently won a much coveted series of races for deep-keel yachts by just $3\frac{1}{2}$ points but he only achieved that by adding $8\frac{1}{2}$ to his over-all total in one go when he expected a breeze and then used the correct tactics when it came. He was able to do this through his knowledge of windcraft.

Over a period of years through studying the wind — by being at a formative time a professional meteorologist on an island on the South Coast of England completely surrounded by small sailing craft and also by sailing my own dinghy — I have acquired a knowledge of what facets of wind behaviour are really of practical use to those who sail. Only the information that the yachtsman on the spot can recognise and interpret is of any use to him. Dinghy people have no weather charts; no radio forecasts; all they have is their acquired knowledge. In this book the basic facts of Windcraft are clearly illustrated to help people understand the wind and so aid them in sailing their boats better, faster and more safely.

The complete beginner can start on this book, but, as well as the things that others may find too simple, there are, I hope, enough wind wrinkles to be of use to all the sailing fraternity. The approach should appeal to those who find deeper explanations unnecessarily complicated and when they have hoisted this in then they can go on to something more complex — like advanced windcraft.

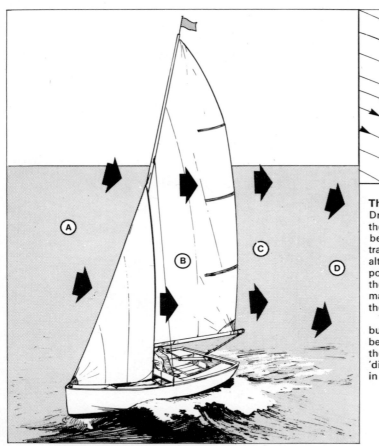

The Boat and the Wind 1

Driving force for sailing comes from part of the total force F exerted by the sails. The force on sails is produced by a difference in pressure between their windward and leeward sides. The wind at (A) is travelling all at one speed and in one direction but the sails make it alter direction and change in speed. The foresail is of particular importance for, together with the mainsail, it forms a slot through which the air must flow. In the slot the air speeds up (B). The faster it can be made to flow compared to the speed on the windward side of the sail the greater the total force F acting.

The sail is efficient if it maintains the flow right across the sail (C), but eventually the wind returns to its former direction (D). Now it will be full of eddies. Only streamline flow will create aerodynamic force on the sails and so the eddies are a hindrance to yachts sailing in the 'dirty wind' (turbulent eddies) of others. Thus a golden rule of sailing in fleets is 'Keep your wind clear'.

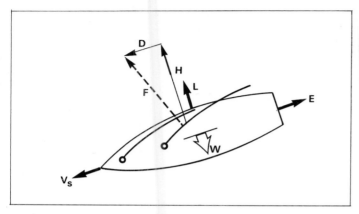

The Boat and the Wind 2

The force F due to the sails can be replaced exactly by two forces at right angles. These are the driving force D which provides forward way and the heeling force H which, were it not for the centreboard, or keel would send the craft scudding off to leeward. The heeling force tends to turn the craft over to leeward and this is counterbalanced by the weight of the crew who provide an opposing righting movement M. The athwartships heeling force H gives the craft a small amount of leeway L. Thus the hull and keel or centreboard are constantly pushing sideways against the water and an opposing force W acts in opposition to the heeling force and this opposes the leeway.

The useful force is the driving force which gives the boat forward way V_s, but experience tells us that the constant application of a force will lead to higher and higher speeds. This does not occur because an opposing drag force E exactly balances the drive force when the boat is sailing at a constant speed. As the wind increases, so drive increases and speed V_s increases until drag again equals drive. You now sail at a higher constant speed. Long thin hulls have less drag which is why catamarans are so efficient.

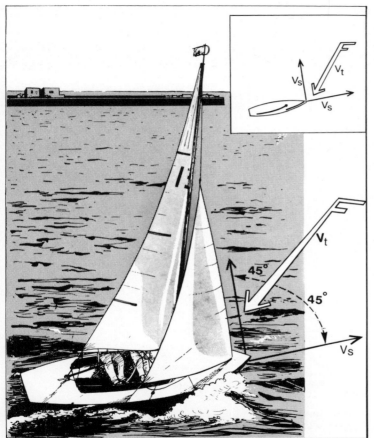

Points of Sailing 1 Close hauled

To sail efficiently to windward you must haul your mainsail and foresail in as far as they will go. You are then 'close hauled', 'beating to windward' or 'on the wind'.

The craft depicted is 'close hauled on the port tack' as the wind V_t is blowing in over its port side. You will see that the boom is hauled down close to the centre-line of the boat (something you must not do on small dinghies) and the bag in the foot of the mainsail allows the sail to belly. V_s is the boat's forward speed.

With a boat heeling like this one it is obvious what is meant by 'putting the helm down'. By so doing the helmsman will bring the boat's bow into and through the wind direction until he is 'close hauled on the starboard tack'. He will then be sailing a course roughly 90° from his original course.

As he was as close to the wind as he could be on the port tack and is now as close to the wind as possible on the starboard tack the sector of directions between is full of impossible sailing directions. So we will call it the 'impossible sector'.

When learning look for a marker before you tack (the buildings on the sea wall in this case) that is dead behind you. After the temporary confusion of coming about on to the new tack, sail first of all for that marker and then correct your course at your leisure.

Sailing close hauled is the most difficult point of sailing. At the same time it is the most rewarding to those who have mastered the technique. The major reason for this is that the instantaneous wind V_i is always shifting and the efficient helmsman reacts to as many of these shifts as he can.

Points of Sailing 2   Close Reaching

For dinghies, close reaching is the fastest point of sailing. In marginal conditions you are more likely to induce the boat to plane on this point of sailing than any other.

The reason for this is that the wind you feel, which is the apparent wind V_a, (not shown) is added to in speed and shifted forward in direction by the boat's forward speed V_s. As V_s is greatest on this point of sailing so for a given true wind V_i the wind the sails feel and react to (again the apparent wind) is greatest for that true wind speed.

It is often an exhilerating point of sailing for every time the wind gusts above 10 to 12 knots dinghies of fourteen feet (4m.) and longer will either plane or attempt to. In stronger winds planing may be almost continuous and then the shorter planing dinghies will plane as well.

Inducing a reluctant dinghy to plane and then coaxing it into holding that plane longer than the others when only the gusts are strong enough to make the boat plane is a technique that separates the experienced helmsman and his crew from the beginners. It means both helmsman and crew easing sheets and then hardening in on them as the wind speed and direction vary. It is a complex technique and to do it efficiently may be the hardest thing that a helmsman and crew have to learn.

At this stage there are no simple rules. Give the boat its head, sit her up, shift your weight aft when she planes and raise your centreplate a quarter or so. Then play it as it comes and in gusty conditions it will come in many shifts of strength and direction.

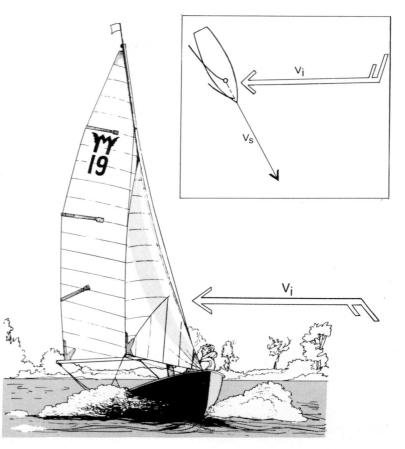

Points of Sailing 3　Broad Reaching

On this point of sailing the wind you feel – the apparent wind V_a – comes from abeam or close to it. Therefore the true wind V_t must come from abaft the beam. This point of sailing is not quite as fast for most dinghies as close reaching since the boat's forward speed V_s does not add so much to the apparent wind V_a on the broad reach as on the close reach.

Sailing with the wind in this position is often referred to as 'having a soldier's wind' so throwing up the old antagonism between the navy and the army. In many old sailing craft the ease of sailing did indeed make the broad reach something that even a soldier could cope with without mishap, but to coax the best out of a modern dinghy or yacht requires the same constant attention on this point of sailing as is required for sailing to windward. In fact more so because there are no absolute pointers such as a fluttering foresail luff to warn when the sails are not meeting the wind at the correct angle of attack.

In the drawing the two boys have adopted the correct positions for planing on a broad reach when the wind is not too strong. They are both bringing their weight further aft than when close hauled but not too far. Only when the stern wave is obviously well clear of the transom will they need to sit still further aft. They are also jockeying their combined weights to hold the boat upright whatever the variations in wind strength.

Points of Sailing 4   Running

When the wind is from a point so far aft that the foresail will not draw or back-winds then the boat is running before the wind. Spinnakers are carried with no difficulty at all and, to balance the boat, helmsman and crew sit on opposite sides. Craft with centreboards lift them to reduce drag on this point of sailing although when there are considerable waves the plate should be left down a third to reduce rolling.

In gusty conditions, when the wind is likely to increase suddenly and shift at the same time (represented by the double arrow), care must be taken to ensure that the wind does not get on the far side of the sail and cause a sudden jibe for which you are not prepared.

Sailing before the wind may be the most difficult of all points of sailing because other boats blanket you and other boats seem to go faster than you do.

Advanced sailors may tack down wind and make more way.

11

Seeing the Wind 1

As the wind itself is invisible so everything we know about it is inferred from watching things that the wind effects.

One of the best indications of wind speed is the tree-tops. When you are worried about the wind being too strong for you or your crew then watch the way the leafy tops succumb to the wind. You will soon come to recognise what degree of motion up there indicates too much wind, or strength very close to the limit. Pages 18 to 21 will help in assessing the actual wind force on the water when you get to the shore or club-house.

Before going sailing observe the wind direction in the open. Use the various aids that exist such as wind-vanes, flags, smoke and even a wetted finger when the wind is light. When it is stronger noting the way trees give to the wind in positions that are well exposed can help to save a capsize as you break clear of the shoreside hamper into the open water.

It helps greatly to have a reference point on the leeward horizon towards which the wind is blowing; or on the windward horizon from which it is blowing. If this landmark is some miles away on a local sailing spree you can use it to mark the wind direction wherever you are sailing.

Seeing the Wind 2

1) When you start to sail the completely new scene that greets you every time you tack can be disconcerting. Sort out from where on the shore the wind is coming and it will still be coming from that same place (P) after you have tacked. If you are tacking, that reference point on the shore, a handy buoy or an anchored boat etc., is the point you should eventually reach.

2) When sailing to windward the experienced helmsman judges the wind by concentrating on the luff of his foresail. He constantly edges his craft towards the wind, eating into it until he sees the luff tremble. Then he instinctively, but gently, pulls his tiller towards him so that the craft curves away from the wind and the luff stiffens again. In this way he undulates through the 'wind cells'. The wind is kind. Even a small wind cell gives you seconds of precious time to make the necessary corrections of course.

The beginner must, as soon as he is able, start to emulate the experienced helmsman and steer an undulating course as close to the wind as he can get without his foresail luff backwinding, but remember 'There's a luff in a puff'.

2

Stay close to the wind

The wind is always varying in speed and direction and so at any moment you sail to an instantaneous wind V_i. When attempting to sail the best course close to the wind you must constantly react to the instantaneous small shifts. To do this always ask your boat to point as close to the wind as it will go without the luff of the foresail shaking or shivering. A shivering luff is, in most craft, the best way of noting when you are too close to the wind.

To keep your boat travelling at its highest forward speed V_s the instantaneous true wind has to be kept at about 45° to the heading of the boat. As the wind V_i shifts about its mean direction so a well-helmed craft sails an undulating course to keep the heading always about 45° to the true wind at the moment.

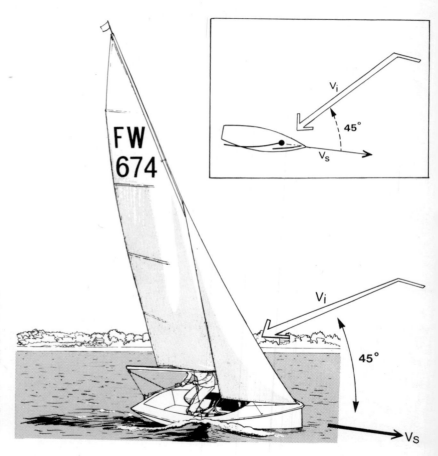

14

y Sail your Boat Upright?

o beginners it may seem fun to sail the boat on its ear. You really
t be going if the wind (W) is pushing you over like this. Not a bit
! The drive force (T) on your sails acts perpendicular to the sail so
n your boat heels you are reducing useful drive (D) and adding a
e (S) whose only action is to push the boat down into the water. If
always sail to keep your boat upright all the drive force acts to help
make way.

ere the crew is not quite doing his best. He is using all his sitting-out
er, but has not remembered to slack off his foresail. The helmsman
illing wind but his efforts are in vain when the foresail is so tightly
ted.

2 This pair are a good team. Both foresail and mainsail are trimmed to
complement one another. The mainsail is well slacked off so that the
useful drive component (D) is directed as far ahead as possible. The
mast is vertical so there is no component of the drive force trying to
sink the boat. They should play sheets to keep the boat upright at all
times and the crew must follow the helmsman, easing to the puffs and
hardening in when the wind eases.

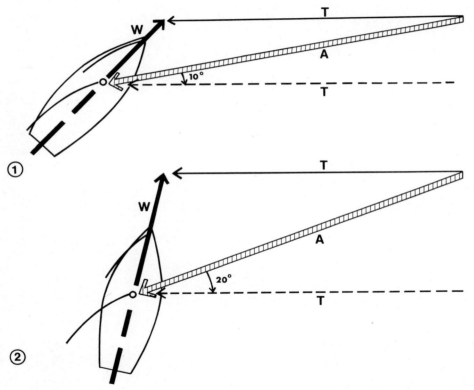

① ②

Where is the True Wind?
Answer:—
10° abaft the apparent wind when beating
20° abaft the apparent wind when reaching

Such a simple rule is obviously rough, but it i
a dinghy crew's rule of thumb. As wind increase
so does boat speed (W) and little change occur
in the angle between true wind (T) and apparer
wind (A). Also fast long dinghies do not make
very appreciable alteration to the rules. The tru
wind will be slightly further aft of the apparer
but not much.

When off the wind the rule assumes that th
dinghy planes or that its off-wind performanc
is a real advance on its close-hauled performanc
These rules may not apply to deep-keel yacht
whose performance on all points is much th
same.

Once the angle between the craft heading (W
and the true wind (T) increases as you free o
the wind, the rule no longer applies beyond th
point where there is a right angle betwee
(W) and (T).

Using the Racing Flag

The flag carried at the masthead is the most important means of judging the wind direction. In light airs it may be the only means. So always carry a masthead flag.

On the wind, keeping the luff of the foresail just stiff shows whether or not you are close to the wind. Off the wind only the masthead flag can truly tell you where the wind is.

In a variable wind the crew watches for collisions. The helmsman should spend time watching the flag and responding to its every shift.

2 The wind you feel is not the true wind — it is the apparent wind A. The true wind direction T is always further aft than the apparent wind which affects the flag.

The wind that results from adding your boat velocity (V_s knots) to the true wind velocity (T knots) is the apparent wind velocity (A knots).

V_s and T have to be added as vectors to give the apparent wind A. Until the true wind comes aft of the beam the apparent wind is stronger than the true wind. A comes before T, i.e. the apparent wind is always further ahead.

3 The masthead flag will always stream in the apparent wind and not the true wind except when running before the wind.

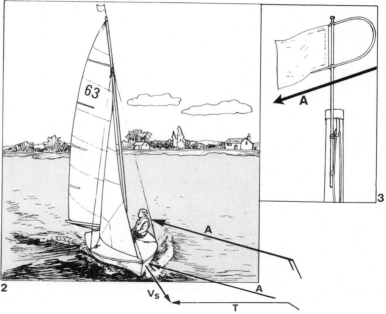

Very Light Winds
Force 0–2 (0–6 knots)

Calms and light airs are relatively rare. When they occur it is often in the early morning or the evening. Dense obstructions can reduce the wind speed to these low values even with moderate winds. Low wind speeds are more likely inland than on the coast.

1   Calm or light air (3 knots or less) The water reflects a glassy image of the craft, or scaley wavelets form. To give the sails a cant and make them set properly you have to sit with your weight slightly to leeward. To make maximum speed in the conditions balance the boat fore-and-aft and keep the greatest length in the water. Sit very still. If you can get the boat moving then try to keep her moving even if it is not quite in the right direction. Her motion creates its own wind – try to keep that wind. In these conditions the racing flag may not respond.

2   Light breeze (4–6 knots). With this wind speed the sails will naturally fill with the wind pressure. The weight of crew and helmsman can be distributed to just keep the boat upright. Small wavelets form and break up the glassy appearance of light airs. Sitting still and concentrating are still essential and any tendency to sheet in as far as with stronger winds should be avoided. Flow must be put into both sails and that means tender care in sheeting them to give as full a belly as they will take. Sometimes it will be possible for both crew members to sit on the windward side.

Gentle to Moderate Winds
Force 3–4 (7–16 knots)

These are the wind speeds you are most likely to have when sailing. They are the most prevalent and light mornings grow to these values by afternoon on many days of the year. They are the winds which are best for learning to sail because the boat responds and you get the feel of it. Planing dinghies manage to plane easily in Force 4 and may do so in Force 3. Force 4 is considered to be the best working breeze for all craft regardless of shape and size.

1 Force 3 Gentle Breeze (7–10 knots) Judge this wind speed at the club house or from yachts flying flags at their moorings because light flags are just extended by it. On the open water 10 knots can just produce a few white horses but on restricted waters you judge this speed from the ease with which you sit the boat up and yet she slices through the water at a fair rate. Modern dinghies love this wind. The longer ones can plane off the wind. The racing flag can be relied on to give the apparent wind direction.

2 Force 4 Moderate Breeze (11–16 knots) This is the wind in which dinghies delight and yet it may be too strong for the real beginner in a tender racing dinghy. However experienced crews love it for there is the real feel of making way to windward. Bear away from the wind and the craft planes away. Both crew members sit out, or the crew stands out on the trapeze, to keep the boat upright when going to windward or on a close reach. On open water the wind can raise a fair smattering of white horses and there are real waves even if they are small.

Fresh to Strong Breezes
Force 5–6 (17–27 knots)

These winds are not for beginners and even with the experienced there will be many capsizes. Beginners with some experience can manage Force 5 in creeks at low water where the flats do not induce much turbulence in the wind. The Force 5 referred to means the wind speed measured in the open where the force is not cut greatly by obstructions.

1 Force 5 Fresh Breeze (17–21 knots) Both crew members will be using all their skill to keep the boat upright. Helmsman and crew must ease sheets to relieve the pressure cn the sails in the gusts associated with this wind speed. This is definitely not a wind in which to relieve the wear-and-tear on your hands by cleating the foresheet. However that does not preclude the use of jam-cleats. Off the wind dinghies take off on screaming planes and care has to be taken to play the waves as well as the wind. Even experienced crews must expect to capsize every so often. From the club-house you can see whether or not the waves are breaking on relatively sheltered waters. If they are the wind is force 5. Small trees in the open sway noticeably.

2 Force 6 Strong Breeze (22–27 knots) Racing dinghies which do not reef are overpowered in this wind speed. This is where yacht gales start and all but the most experienced will think twice before they go out. The speeds quoted are mean speed and take no account of the gusts (See page 22).

This wind whistles through wires and makes quite large branches sway noticeably. On the open sea the waves are becoming large, dinghies can lose sight of each other below the wave crests. On no account should beignners think of going out·and if caught out lower mainsail and come home under foresail only.

Beaufort Scale of Wind Force

Beaufort No.	General Description	Sea Criterion	Landsman's Criterion	Limits of velocity in knots
0	Calm	Sea like a mirror.	Calm; smoke rises vertically.	Less than 1
1	Light air	Ripples with the appearance of scales are formed, but without foam crests.	Direction of wind shown by smoke drift but not by wind vanes.	1 to 3
2	Light breeze	Small wavelets, still short but more pronounced. Crests have a glassy appearance and do not break.	Wind felt on face; leaves rustle; ordinary vane moved by wind.	4 to 6
3	Gentle breeze	Large wavelets. Crests begin to break. Foam of glassy appearance. Perhaps scattered white horses.	Leaves and small twigs in constant motion. Wind extends light flags.	7 to 10
4	Moderate breeze	Small waves becoming longer; fairly frequent white horses.	Raises dust and loose paper; small branches are moved.	11 to 16
5	Fresh breeze	Moderate waves, taking a more pronounced long form; many white horses are formed. Chance of some spray.	Small trees in leaf begin to sway. Crested wavelets form on inland waters.	17 to 21
6	Strong breeze	Large waves begin to form; the white foam crests are more extensive everywhere. Probably some spray.	Large branches in motion; whistling heard in telegraph wires, umbrellas used with difficulty.	22 to 27
7	Near gale	Sea heaps up and white foam from breaking waves begins to be blown in streaks along the direction of the wind.	Whole trees in motion; inconvenience felt when walking against wind.	28 to 33
8	Gale	Moderately high waves of greater length; edges of crests begin to break into spindrift. The foam is blown in well-marked streaks along the direction of the wind.	Breaks twigs off trees; generally impedes progress.	34 to 40
9	Strong gale	High waves. Dense streaks of foam along the direction of the wind. Crests of waves begin to topple, tumble and roll over. Spray may affect visibility	Slight structural damage occurs (chimney-pots and slates removed).	41 to 47
10	Storm	Very high waves with long over-hanging crests. The resulting foam in great patches is blown in dense white streaks along the direction of the wind. On the whole the surface takes on a white appearance. The tumbling of the sea becomes heavy and shock-like. Visibility affected.	Seldom experienced inland; trees uprooted considerable structural damage occurs.	48 to 55

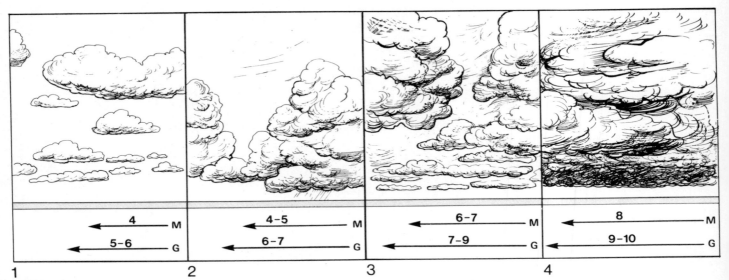

	4	M		4–5	M		6–7	M		8	M
	5–6	G		6–7	G		7–9	G		9–10	G

1   2   3   4

Add the Gusts

1 Moderate wind speed with low layer clouds does not produce much gustiness, but there are turbulent overturnings. However with cumulus-type clouds Force 4 mean speed regularly becomes Force 5–6 in the gusts. The gusts do not last long, but while they are there they have to be met by hard-sitting out or standing out on a trapeze, or if the gust is too strong, by easing sheets and spilling wind. That means foresheet as well as main.

2 When heap clouds grow big then they haul down wind from higher up and the gusts are stronger. The mean speed may be only force 4–5, but the gusts especially in showers may be Force 6–8. Both dinghies and larger craft should allow for the gusts when showers are forecast or when large cumulus or cumulonimbus clouds are evident. Remember that Cu and Force 3–4 in the morning will probably mean showers and Force 4–5 (mean speed) by the afternoon.

3 When the weather is cyclonic (i.e. the nasty weather that occurs near the centres of depressions or in troughs of low pressure) then lumpiness in the lower sky indicates strong gusts. The wind may already be Force 6–7 and so the gusts can be Force 7–9. The gusts often come with a roll or a line of low cloud and may herald a clearance after which it blows hard, but from a sky more like (z).

4 When the weather is really bad, features of the wind regime flash by at high speed driven by the gale-force winds. If wind is gale force at the surface it is more than gale force aloft. When that wind comes down, as it does in big eddies, then roll-like clouds form and the wind may locally increase to force 9–10 and in extreme cases force 11. The force 10 gusts are not likely to be sustained but they have to be weathered and an over-canvassed craft could be in real trouble.

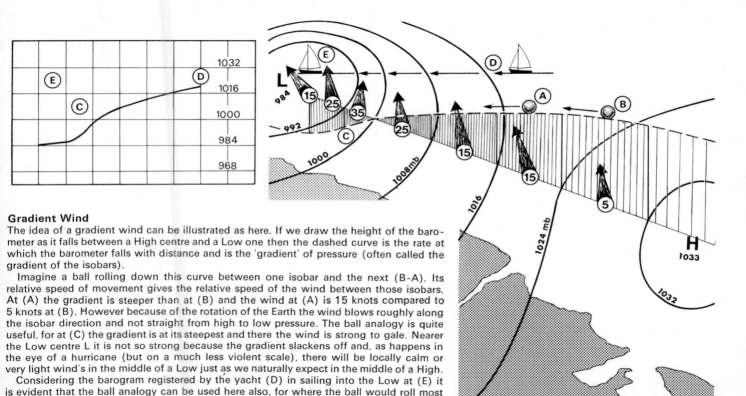

Gradient Wind

The idea of a gradient wind can be illustrated as here. If we draw the height of the barometer as it falls between a High centre and a Low one then the dashed curve is the rate at which the barometer falls with distance and is the 'gradient' of pressure (often called the gradient of the isobars).

Imagine a ball rolling down this curve between one isobar and the next (B-A). Its relative speed of movement gives the relative speed of the wind between those isobars. At (A) the gradient is steeper than at (B) and the wind at (A) is 15 knots compared to 5 knots at (B). However because of the rotation of the Earth the wind blows roughly along the isobar direction and not straight from high to low pressure. The ball analogy is quite useful, for at (C) the gradient is at its steepest and the wind is strong to gale. Nearer the Low centre L it is not so strong because the gradient slackens off and, as happens in the eye of a hurricane (but on a much less violent scale), there will be locally calm or very light wind's in the middle of a Low just as we naturally expect in the middle of a High.

Considering the barogram registered by the yacht (D) in sailing into the Low at (E) it is evident that the ball analogy can be used here also, for where the ball would roll most rapidly down the trace is where the strong wind is. (Note: time on this barogram runs from right to left).

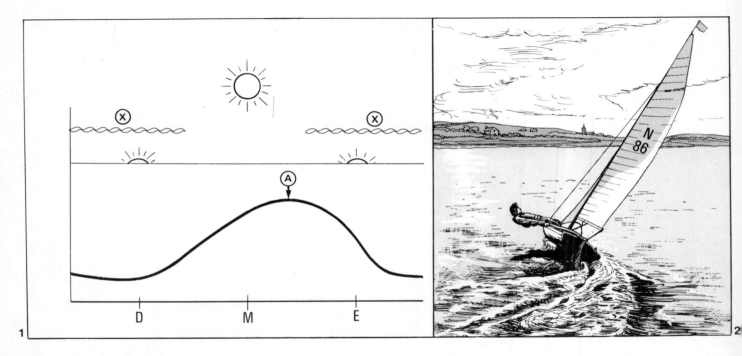

Wind Speed through the Day

1 Wind speed is lowest around dawn D. Soon it begins to rise and climbs to a maximum (A) an hour or two after local noon M. The wind sinks with the sun, E rapidly falls losing speed in the evening. It may even go temporarily calm. These variations are associated with fair weather over ·or near land. However, it is noticeable that whatever the weather conditions these trends appear—the wind tries to be least by night and greatest in the afternoon. It appears suddenly in the morning when the inversion layer (X) breaks (the 'thermal lid' that has formed over land by night) and dies suddenly in the evening or late afternoon when it re-forms (X).

Morning

2 In the morning the typical strength may be Force 2–3 (5–10kt) but the morning wind can be the most variable of the day. In the drawing the state of sea indicates a low average wind speed, but there is a sudden gust. This is typical of morning variability.

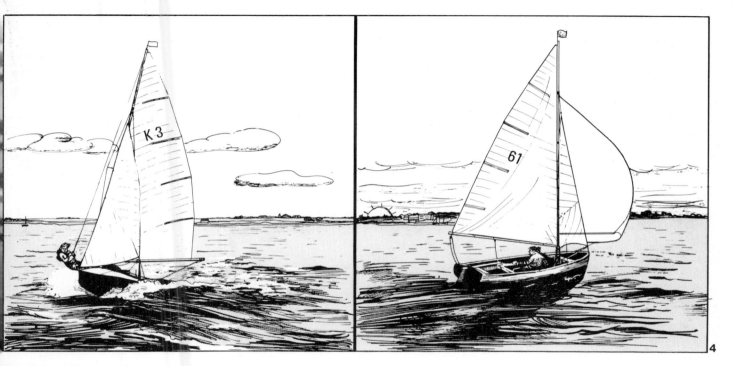

Wind Speed Through the Day 2
3 Afternoon

In the afternoon the wind is normally at its strongest, but least variable. What may be typically Force 2–3 in the morning becomes 4–5 in the afternoon. This leads to almost continuous planing by the longer dinghies and to planing off the wind by shorter ones.

4 Evening

When the sun sinks towards the horizon the wind begins to decrease in speed and Force 4–5 in the afternoon can fall as low as 2–3, or even to 0–2, when fully under the influence of land. The wind temporarily becomes less variable with evening but may resume its variability during the night. Odd spikes sometimes appear in the overnight wind – a reason for carrying less canvass by night than by day under the same conditions.

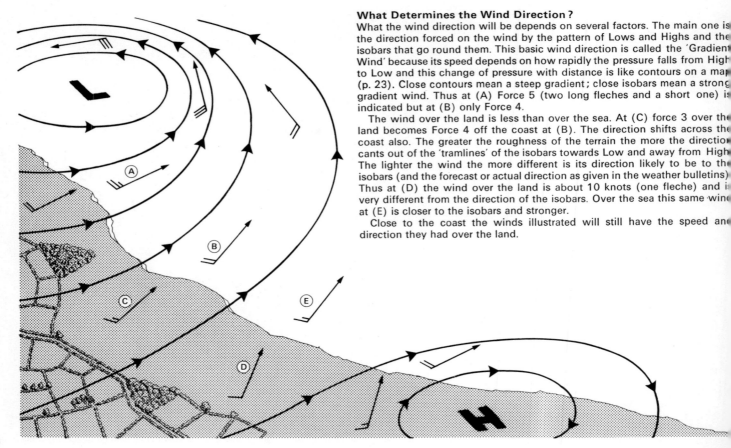

What Determines the Wind Direction?

What the wind direction will be depends on several factors. The main one is the direction forced on the wind by the pattern of Lows and Highs and the isobars that go round them. This basic wind direction is called the 'Gradient Wind' because its speed depends on how rapidly the pressure falls from High to Low and this change of pressure with distance is like contours on a map (p. 23). Close contours mean a steep gradient; close isobars mean a strong gradient wind. Thus at (A) Force 5 (two long fleches and a short one) is indicated but at (B) only Force 4.

The wind over the land is less than over the sea. At (C) force 3 over the land becomes Force 4 off the coast at (B). The direction shifts across the coast also. The greater the roughness of the terrain the more the direction cants out of the 'tramlines' of the isobars towards Low and away from High. The lighter the wind the more different is its direction likely to be to the isobars (and the forecast or actual direction as given in the weather bulletins). Thus at (D) the wind over the land is about 10 knots (one fleche) and is very different from the direction of the isobars. Over the sea this same wind at (E) is closer to the isobars and stronger.

Close to the coast the winds illustrated will still have the speed and direction they had over the land.

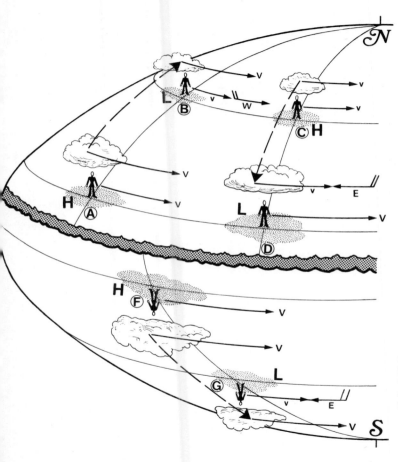

How the Rotation of the Earth alters the Wind Direction

Air will flow from where pressure is high H to where it is low L. So winds should blow straight from high to low? Not true because of the rotation of the Earth. On the equator of the spinning ball that is the Earth you travel eastwards at about 1000 miles per hour (about 1600 km/hr). As you move towards the pole your rate of eastward travel slows down until at the pole you just rotate on the spot once every 24 hours.

So at (A) assume the wind is calm in the middle of a High and both you and the air are travelling eastwards at high speed V. However the air sees low pressure to the north and moves towards it. The air parcel is not fixed to the Earth so it goes on travelling at V.

Another observer (B) in the Low is only moving with the Earth at lower speed V and the free air travels past him as a wind from the west W. So air that moves northwards turns into a west wind.

Conversely observer in a High at (C) is travelling at speed V and so is the air. There is no relative motion between them. The air moves south towards low retaining its eastward speed of V, but the observer at (D) fixed to the Earth is travelling at the higher speed V. Therefore he feels an easterly wind E.

This leads to the rule

Stand back to the wind in the Northern Hemisphere and Pressure is Low on your Left

In the southern hemisphere the air and observer at (F) are travelling at the higher speed V eastwards where the pressure is high. The air moves towards low pressure retaining its speed, while the earth slows down beneath it (G). The result is easterly wind and the above rule now modifies to Stand *facing* the wind and pressure is Low on your Left.

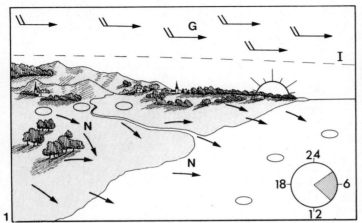

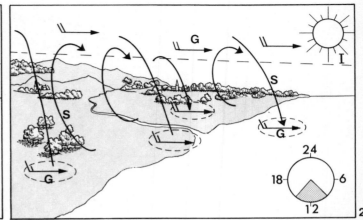

Wind Shifts During the Day 1

Forecast 'Winds will be light to moderate or light variable.' Near the coast on days with light to moderate winds there are often four distinct regimes of wind direction that follow one another as the day progresses. **Early Morning** Around dawn, and for a few hours afterwards, the most likely wind direction is from the land. It will be very light in most instances – the ghost of the nocturnal wind N that has blown off the land during the night. This post-dawn period is when wind-making forces are at their least over the land. The surface air is sluggish as it has to contend with things in its path such as woods and houses etc. The gradient wind G is locked away above a temperature inversion I that forms over land during the night. The surface wind cannot pick up until the sun has broken the inversion, and there are many calms. **2 Forenoon** During the morning, and usually before 10 or 11 a.m., the sun can cut through the inversion layer. Then the second wind of the day appears, sweeping away the wind of early morning. This new wind is likely to be light to moderate and from some direction different from the morning wind. What has happened is that the wind that was above the inversion (the gradient wind G) is brought in chunks down to the surface by thermals. This speeds up the surface wind S but it is often a very variable wind with many direction and speed changes in it. However if the sun continues to shine and the wind is not already from the sea then look out for the next major wind – the sea breeze.

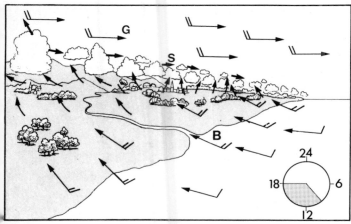

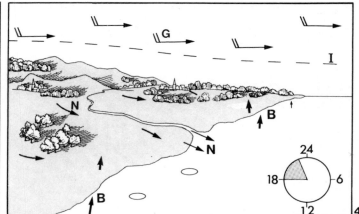

Wind Shifts During the Day 2

Forecast 'Winds will be light to moderate – chance of seabreezes'

3 Afternoon By lunch time the forenoon wind can often be replaced by a wind from the sea. This is the seabreeze B – a phenomenon of all coasts when the sun shines and winds are light to moderate. In calm conditions the seabreeze can appear by breakfast time near the coast but when there is a moderate wind S opposing it it may not stagger onto the shore before the afternoon. When the seabreeze does arrive it usually stays and there is a steady sailing breeze off the sea for the afternoon. On days with stronger winds or days when cloud cuts the sun from the land the forenoon wind stays (with some variations) all day. In any case the onset of evening will bring the last wind regime of the day.

4 Evening As soon as the sun has really begun to sink the inversion I re-forms. When it does so surface winds fall light or even calm. Whatever the wind it will tend to become lighter when evening approaches and often changes its direction from its afternoon direction. The last of the seabreeze will usually veer and be gone by dusk and then there will be a calmish patch until the first of the nocturnal wind N begins to seep off the land. In all of the above you have to assume that no large scale pressure pattern changes are going to come along during the day – the forecast should warn of any change in the gradient wind direction G.

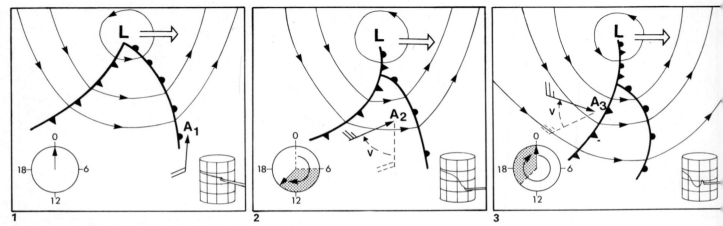

1 **2** **3**

Long Period Wind Shifts – When Troughs Pass

Forecast A trough of low pressure will cross the area. **Meaning** The wind direction may shift back into the south at first but it will veer, west to northwest later.

When the typical northern hemisphere depression passes then one or more troughs of low pressure pass across a sailing venue A_1.

1 The typical wind direction ahead of the trough is southerly (which includes SE to SW) and typical wind speed is 15 to 20 knots. The barometer should be falling but not very steeply. The time indicated is zero at the moment and typical elapsed times are shown for subsequent phases of the shift pattern.

If the barometer should dive very steeply then anticipate gale force winds soon.

2 As the low tracks by to the north of the position A_2 the barometer will fall to its lowest and steady off at the time of passage of the trough. This period of lowest pressure may be characterised by frontal weather, i.e. the weather is at its worst compared to what has preceded it or

will follow it. In only a very few troughs is the weather very bad. Mos troughs are characterised by increasing cloudiness, rain that intensifie and some wind increase, but it may not get above Force 5–6. There ma be a sudden squall and a shift of wind as the trough passes. This characteristic of a frontal trough.

3 The wind veers either gradually with time or in a series of shift Typically 6 to 12 hours elapses between the situations shown.

As the trough recedes so the wind will go on veering A_3. The weathe type will usually change to polar air sometimes with showers. Hea clouds characterise this period.

The typical rise in the barometer is a moderate one that maintains i rate for some time, indicating a ridge of high pressure moving in. Th phase may occur as much as 24 hours after A_1. If the barometer rise sharply and then steadies while heap clouds either die out or increase t cover whole sky anticipate stronger wind to come.

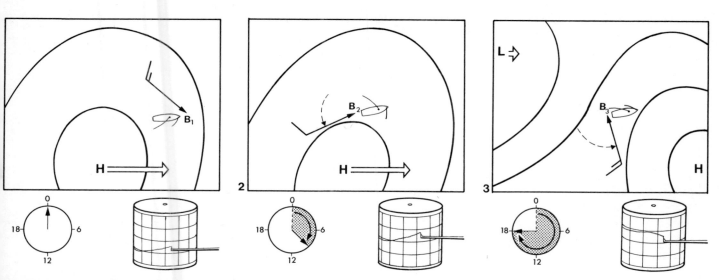

Long Period Wind Shifts – When Ridges Pass

When a ridge of high pressure travels across an area it often does so between two depressions and the typical time for the sequence of shifts shown is 20 hours or so. At the time 1 the wind is typically NW 15kt. The most likely temperate latitudes situation is shown with a recent history of a depression that has passed. Skies are now clearing and pressure is rising steadily.

Some hours later the ridge axis overtakes even a yacht running before the wind. The later has steadily backed (shifted anticlockwise) and decreased to say 5–10 knots. It could stick there and this would indicate a spell of fair weather.

However in a run of depressions the most likely event is that the wind will go on backing into the south with a gradual fall of pressure that speeds up with time. The wind will probably increase and signs of a new depression may appear in the sky and on the barometer. Weather will usually be fair throughout the period.

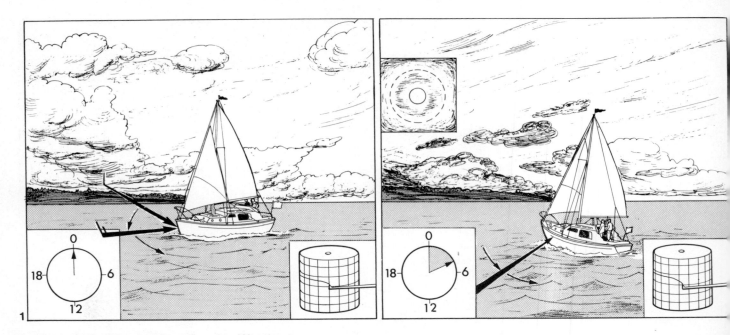

Backing Shifts Ahead of Deteriorating Weather

1 First signs of a backing wind ahead of deteriorating weather are streaks of cirrus cloud moving in above cumulus cloud. Wind direction is typically W to NW and may at this early time show no sign yet of shifting back towards S. Barometer may not show any real tendency to fall. The time that typically must elapse before this backing (and usually increasing) phase is over is 8–12 hours.

2 The next major sky signs are cirrus passing and being replaced by a milky veil of cirrostratus cloud. The box illustrates the halo that forms in such cloud about sun or moon. Average time to passage of a front (and so to a veer in the wind rather than a backing or steady phase) is now 6–9 hours. The wind should now show real signs of backing toward SW if not to S. There may be a strengthening of the wind, but it is usually not marked at this time. The barometer now shows real signs of fall. As this phase progresses darker (altostratus) cloud appears on windward horizon and advances. Cumulus darkens and tends to disperse.

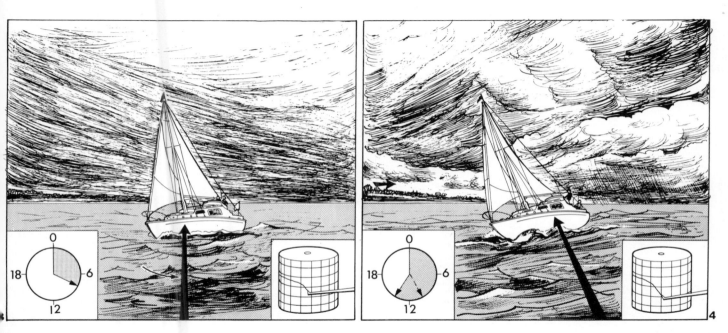

3 Real deterioration is now obvious. Great banks of dark (often flat) cloud advance from windward. Wind backs towards S and may already be there. It can go SE, but may not go back that far. Definite increase now. Darkening sky and sea make it appear worse than it may actually be. Seaway increases. Barometer really falling. If sharp fall then sharp increase in wind – possibly to gale force. If slow fall then less wind and whole backing phase occupies greater time interval. Typical time to elapse before wind veers is now 3–6 hours.

4 Beneath the overcast. The wind has freshened and not shifted much for some time because it has backed as far as it will. Next major wind-shift event is the passage of a front or trough and a veer of wind. Barometer has dropped steadily. May show signs of steadying. When the line of lightening sky appears to windward then expect veer on its passage. Barometer should steady and can rise a little. As depicted the time to the veer is not very long.

For next sequence of events see page 34.

Sudden Veers of Wind – The Passing Warm Front

When a warm front passes then a whole history of developing cloud layers, followed by lowering cloud base and rain, helps to convince that a change must eventually follow. Sight of a break in the otherwise dark windward horizon must be suspected of heralding the passage of the warm front and a more-or-less sudden veer of wind.

The situation depicted in 3 is just behind the warm front (W) whose cloud-wall is receding into the east. The wind at (A) under the rain and low cloud was S or even SE. It is now SW–W (B) and typically is 15–20 kt. There is often a temporary break in the cloud behind the front and then the stratus and stratocumulus clouds (left of the drawing) close in. Drizzle may occur and mist or fog can develop.

The wind shift is to be found under trailing wisps of low cloud (virga) and the barometer which has been falling often steadies as shown on the barogram (2). The yacht's new situation is shown in (1) with the warm front (W) just passed, rain ceased but some drizzle from low cloud. Visibility is poor and the air is humid (muggy).

The next major wind shift usually comes at the cold front.

Sudden Veers of Wind – the passing Cold Front

The approach of a cold front is usually discernible. Basic features are indicated in the drawing. The low cloud line marks the most likely region for a sudden veering shift and there may be sudden rain as well. The cloud wall of the advancing front may sometimes be obscured by low cloud advancing ahead of the front itself, but at other times there is a break ahead of the front that enables its progress to be monitored.

In the case depicted we can look through under the front and see shower clouds building in the cold air behind. The wind which at the moment is from SW must be expected to veer to between W and NW somewhere near the line of trailing low cloud (virga). This sudden shift

and possible increase would need to be watched by a yacht sailing on the point shown. However starboard is the prudent tack to be on for one can round-up to meet the shift when it comes. A yacht on port tack might be put in irons when the wind suddenly shifted ahead.

The weather chart in the region shown will look like (2) with rain and showers to follow the wind shift at (C) and the barogram that steadied off as the warm front (W) passed will begin to rise as the cold front (C) passes. The rise is not a herald of the shift as that has probably already occurred before the barometer shows true signs of rising.

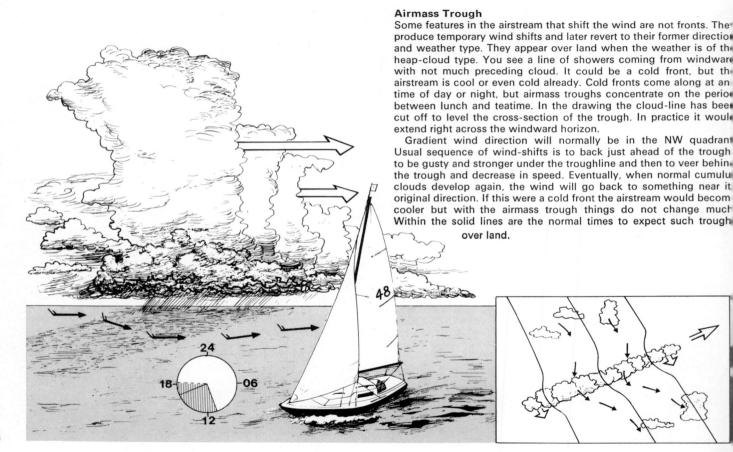

Airmass Trough

Some features in the airstream that shift the wind are not fronts. They produce temporary wind shifts and later revert to their former direction and weather type. They appear over land when the weather is of the heap-cloud type. You see a line of showers coming from windward with not much preceding cloud. It could be a cold front, but the airstream is cool or even cold already. Cold fronts come along at any time of day or night, but airmass troughs concentrate on the period between lunch and teatime. In the drawing the cloud-line has been cut off to level the cross-section of the trough. In practice it would extend right across the windward horizon.

Gradient wind direction will normally be in the NW quadrant. Usual sequence of wind-shifts is to back just ahead of the trough, to be gusty and stronger under the troughline and then to veer behind the trough and decrease in speed. Eventually, when normal cumulus clouds develop again, the wind will go back to something near its original direction. If this were a cold front the airstream would become cooler but with the airmass trough things do not change much. Within the solid lines are the normal times to expect such troughs over land.

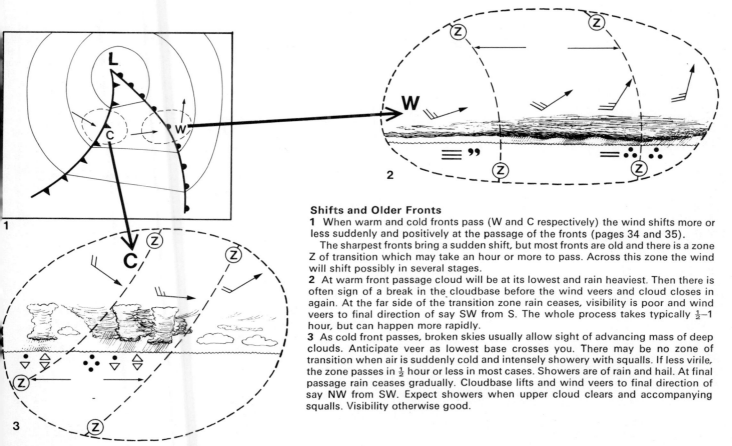

Shifts and Older Fronts

1 When warm and cold fronts pass (W and C respectively) the wind shifts more or less suddenly and positively at the passage of the fronts (pages 34 and 35).

The sharpest fronts bring a sudden shift, but most fronts are old and there is a zone Z of transition which may take an hour or more to pass. Across this zone the wind will shift possibly in several stages.

2 At warm front passage cloud will be at its lowest and rain heaviest. Then there is often sign of a break in the cloudbase before the wind veers and cloud closes in again. At the far side of the transition zone rain ceases, visibility is poor and wind veers to final direction of say SW from S. The whole process takes typically $\frac{1}{2}$–1 hour, but can happen more rapidly.

3 As cold front passes, broken skies usually allow sight of advancing mass of deep clouds. Anticipate veer as lowest base crosses you. There may be no zone of transition when air is suddenly cold and intensely showery with squalls. If less virile, the zone passes in $\frac{1}{2}$ hour or less in most cases. Showers are of rain and hail. At final passage rain ceases gradually. Cloudbase lifts and wind veers to final direction of say NW from SW. Expect showers when upper cloud clears and accompanying squalls. Visibility otherwise good.

Seabreeze Morning

The typical morning when seabreezes will blow is one characterised by

  i) light winds

  ii) clear skies early and cumulus clouds later

The situation depicted is one which provides the most profound wind-shifts. The dinghy is broad-reaching out of the estuary towards the open sea and the wind W is therefore from a point landward. The time is going to be middle or late morning in most cases and there may be signs of the seabreeze already at work near the main coastline. Ships far at sea will not show any signs of the seabreeze for they are well beyond its influence. A sailing boat near the entrance can be seen to be becalmed or nearly so. This signifies that a seabreeze calm C exists over the coastline. That calm will advance inland so the dinghy will soon itself be becalmed. The calm will pass but if the tide is on the flood then hug the shore. The best shore would seem to be the right hand one for it is not sheltered from the wind. However when the calm passes and the seabreeze blows the right hand side is the most likely to be sheltered from the new breeze S off the sea.

    The weather map most likely to produce these conditions is one with a ridge of high pressure over the coasts concerned. As depicted south and east-facing coasts will experience the wind-against-seabreeze effects. The Atlantic westerlies and northwesterlies are the ones that aid the formation of seabreezes most readily by their ability to form heap clouds (cumulus). Breezes covering hundreds of miles of coastline and involving millions of tons of air start up on such mornings and blow for the day.

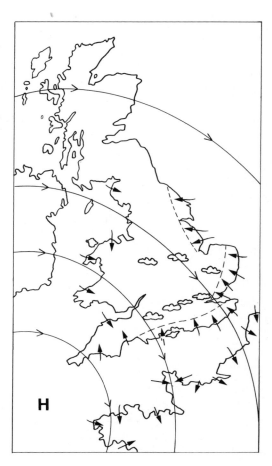

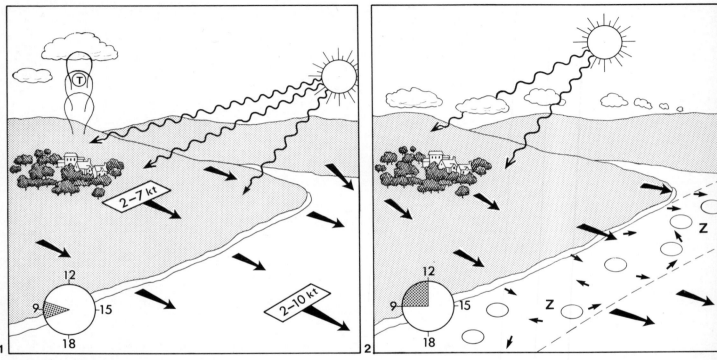

Seabreeze Day

1 The seabreeze effects can begin as soon as the sun heats the land and produces thermals (T). The first visible sign of thermals is the formation of cumulus clouds. (Although clouds do not have to form). This sketch represents the early forenoon of a day when breezes are very likely. The wind at this time should not be more than 6 or 7 knots mean speed and preferably less.

2 Here the seabreeze forces are really at work in the middle of the forenoon. The effect is to reproduce a flat calm (circles) or nearly so over a wide strip of water close to the main coastline. This strip tends to skip across estuaries rather than bend round into them. Cumulus clouds are often quite numerous by now.

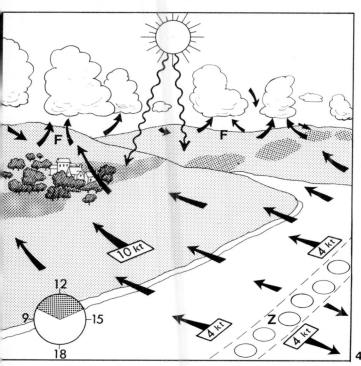

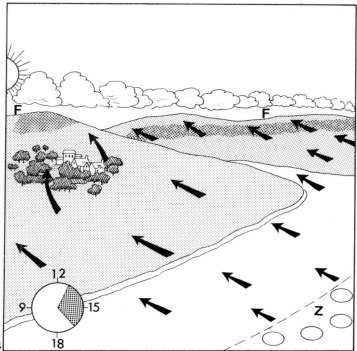

3 The next major event is the invasion of the shore by the seabreeze. This occurs when thermals (and their capping cumulus clouds) form strongly over the hot beachlands. These thermals provide 'chimneys' up which both on-shore seabreeze and opposing off-shore wind can escape. The seabreeze now blows at 10 knots or so. The strengthening force of the breeze thrusts back the opposing wind and the line of division (a seabreeze front F) moves inland.

4 By the afternoon the front is usually well inland and the whole coastal area is visited by a steady seabreeze current. Another effect is to make it quite cloudless over the coast.

Further offshore the outer edge of the coastal calm zone (Z) in (2) has moved out seaward as in (3) and (4). Further seaward the wind will usually be that which existed in the morning.

41

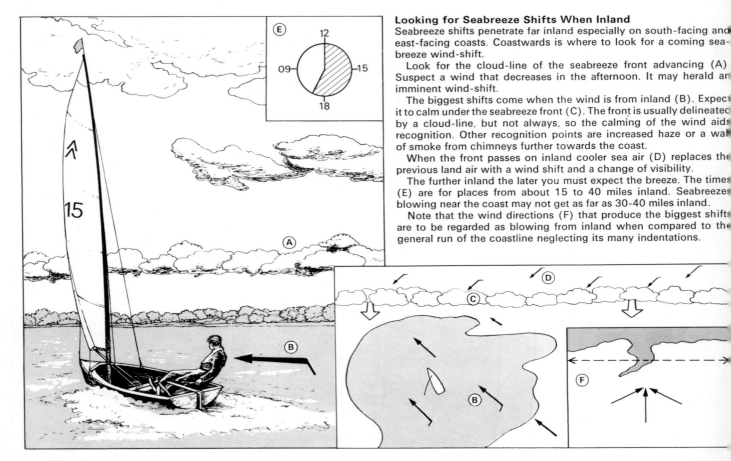

Looking for Seabreeze Shifts When Inland

Seabreeze shifts penetrate far inland especially on south-facing and east-facing coasts. Coastwards is where to look for a coming seabreeze wind-shift.

Look for the cloud-line of the seabreeze front advancing (A). Suspect a wind that decreases in the afternoon. It may herald an imminent wind-shift.

The biggest shifts come when the wind is from inland (B). Expect it to calm under the seabreeze front (C). The front is usually delineated by a cloud-line, but not always, so the calming of the wind aids recognition. Other recognition points are increased haze or a wall of smoke from chimneys further towards the coast.

When the front passes on inland cooler sea air (D) replaces the previous land air with a wind shift and a change of visibility.

The further inland the later you must expect the breeze. The times (E) are for places from about 15 to 40 miles inland. Seabreezes blowing near the coast may not get as far as 30-40 miles inland.

Note that the wind directions (F) that produce the biggest shifts are to be regarded as blowing from inland when compared to the general run of the coastline neglecting its many indentations.

Ways in Which the Seabreeze Sets In

1 In this composite sketch we illustrate the curious things that can happen near the calm zone under the seabreeze front. Seaward is to the extreme right – this is a land-locked waterway. From this direction comes the seabreeze in which the right-hand craft is sailing. On the extreme left the off-shore wind is still blowing lightly. Between them the dinghy is becalmed.

2 On warm gentle days the seabreeze is very sluggish despite the heat. The inversion that keeps it hot also suppresses the seabreeze. So extensive calm may exist along the coastal belt.

3 Sometimes just off the beach the dark-cloud-line of a seabreeze front moves backwards and forwards as the seabreeze fights a moderate off-shore wind. This is usually an afternoon phenomenon. Then the most curious wind-shifts can occur and different directions exist within a short distance of one another.

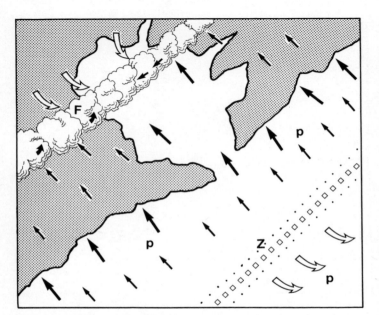

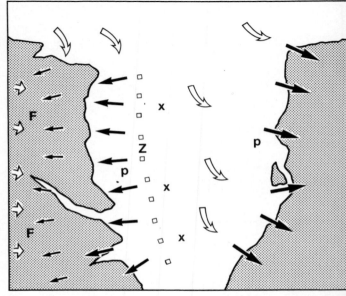

Passage-making – Seabreeze afternoon

On the days when seabreezes blow then there is a calm zone Z somewhere offshore which it is essential to avoid if passage-making along the coast. Thus within a few miles of the coastline, and the closer the better, the strongest wind for passage-making (p) will be found. The calm zone Z may be ten to twenty miles (15–30 km) offshore in the afternoons of good seabreeze days so only if you are further offshore than that can you expect to have a reliable wind for deep-water passage-making.

Seabreezes and Waterways

When the wind at sea is angled to the coasts of a wide waterway (say 50 or more miles wide) the seabreeze regime illustrated can occur. The strength on the windward coast will be less than on the leeward coast and the latter must not be greater than about 15 knots. The seabreeze front system (F) and offshore calm zone (Z) will be found off the sheltered coast while on the opposite coast seabreeze forces will aid the on-shore wind (open arrows) in very often producing fresh winds. Again passage-making is most reliable at p but is unreliable at x.

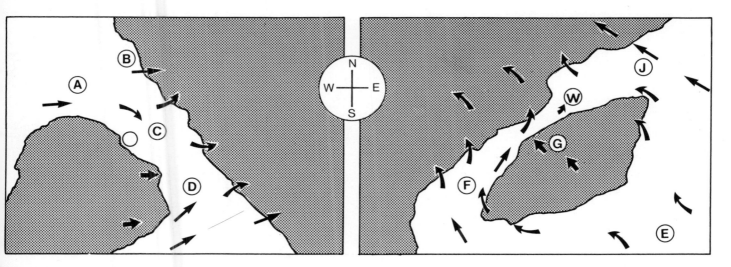

Seabreezes and Islands

When seabreezes can blow it signifies a generally light wind regime. In the left-hand case the general wind (A) is from a westerly point. On the coast (B), that is unfettered by the island, the seabreeze blows ashore without hindrance.

Seabreezes are shallow winds and substantial islands tend to deflect the breeze round them. Thus at (C) there will be wind-starvation unless the breeze pulls in up the channel. On the island side of (C) there may well be frustrating calms. At (D) we have assumed that a little wind comes over a lower end of the island and so 'straightens' the wind flow here. Also the wider channel there allows for less canalisation.

In the right-hand case the undisturbed breeze pulls in from SE and must flow round the island. The channel facing south is favoured and will provide the seabreeze first. It will also canalise the breeze into a stronger overall wind.

This breeze in the southern channel must escape onto the land and may be aided by some wind coming over the island (G). Where the wind splits, between that coming round the north of the island and that coming up the southern channel, there will be a zone of curious winds (W) associated with calms. Where the coast is unfettered (J) the breeze will pull straight ashore towards the hinterland.

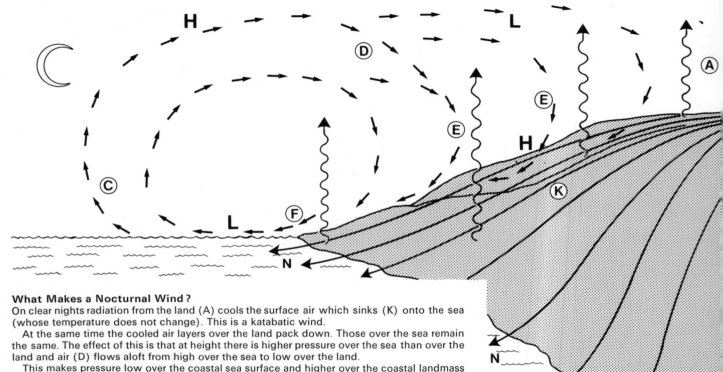

What Makes a Nocturnal Wind?

On clear nights radiation from the land (A) cools the surface air which sinks (K) onto the sea (whose temperature does not change). This is a katabatic wind.

At the same time the cooled air layers over the land pack down. Those over the sea remain the same. The effect of this is that at height there is higher pressure over the sea than over the land and air (D) flows aloft from high over the sea to low over the land.

This makes pressure low over the coastal sea surface and higher over the coastal landmass So air (F) flows from land to sea. This is the landbreeze.

Katabatic+landbreeze=nocturnal wind (N).

Landbreezes occur where there are no hills, but katabatics need sloping ground to the sea. The steeper the slopes the stronger the nocturnal wind.

Cool air off the land (C) must rise over the warmer sea and air must sink (E) over the land and a landbreeze circulation similar to, but weaker than, the seabreeze circulation occurs.

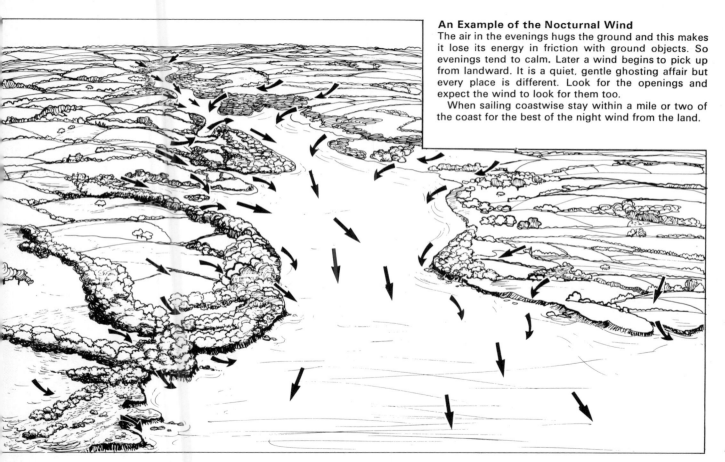

An Example of the Nocturnal Wind

The air in the evenings hugs the ground and this makes it lose its energy in friction with ground objects. So evenings tend to calm. Later a wind begins to pick up from landward. It is a quiet, gentle ghosting affair but every place is different. Look for the openings and expect the wind to look for them too.

When sailing coastwise stay within a mile or two of the coast for the best of the night wind from the land.

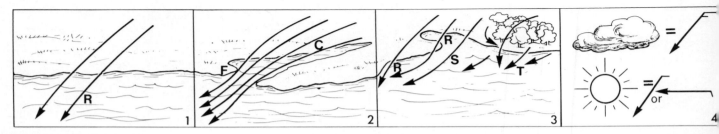

Wind Along the Shore

Here we illustrate the shifts that can occur close to shore. There are so many possibilities that only principles can be stated and the helmsman on the spot must decide how to handle the shifts.

1 When winds are off-shore the drag of the land slows the wind. When it can escape over water it speeds up, causing the refraction effect (R).

2 Where waterways come more closely parallel to the wind directior canalisation (C) occurs along them and air will take the easiest road t the sea. A funnelling effect (F) may occur in the entrance.

3 A promontary produces a steering effect (S) where the streamline try to wrap round the projection. Shoreside copses or woods produc wind shadows (p. 52) and turbulence effects (T).

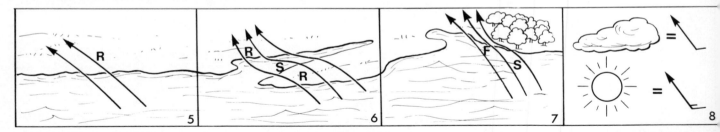

4 When it is cloudy over the land then there is no thermal effect on the off-shore wind direction. When it is sunny the effect is to slow the wind or shift it closer to the shore. However also allow for seabreezes.

5 When the wind is on-shore the refraction effect (R) need not affect the shoreside water at all.

6 The refraction effect could still be in the wind that has crossed a narrow neck of land and then escapes again onto the water. There will be the same steering effect (S) as when the wind is off-shore. Canalisation and funnelling must be allowed for.

7 The effect of shoreside obstructions is felt for about ten times th height of the obstruction to windward so a steering effect (S) can occ and for a surprising way off. Funnelling can also occur round the end the obstructions and leads to local increases in speed.

8 When it is sunny the effect is to enhance the on-shore wind speed an possibly shift the direction more shorewards. This thermal effect must b added to other shoreside effects.

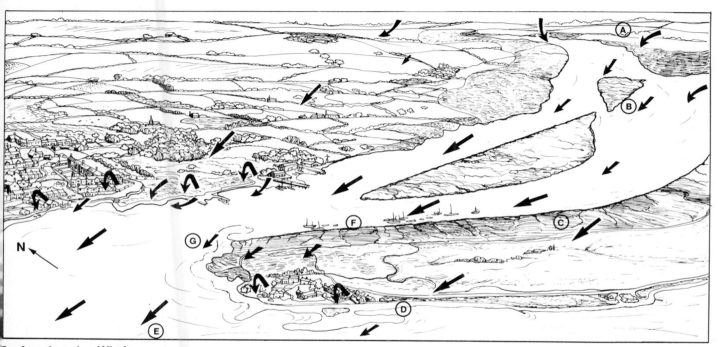

Surface-hugging Winds

The flat-floors of creeks rivers etc. will always tend to steer winds along them. It may seem that coastal mud-flats, sand-bars etc. are low and smooth and perhaps would have little effect on the wind direction. This is not so, particularly in the mornings and evenings; during the night; whenever the sky is low overcast and when the wind is not above moderate.

The wind at (A) is easterly. It will tend to flow along the creeks and be divided by an island such as (B). When forced to leave water for land the direction shifts more landward (C). The momentum of the air leaving the land at (D) leads to it continuing to maintain this direction of east over the water at (E).

Air coming down two channels as at (F) must find 'room' by blowing across the point between (F) and (G) and turbulent eddies will occur in it from the coastal complex of houses etc. between (D) and (G). Similarly eddies will occur over the boatyards and slipways of the town leading to local gusts and calms and also shifts of direction.

Coastal Slope and Mistral/Bora Type Winds

1 High ground inland, and especially snow-capped mountains, induce strong to gale force winds over coastal waters. These are highly developed katabatic winds usually aided by gradient winds (G) in the same direction i.e. from over the mountains.

They are found particularly along the coasts of the Gulf of Lions and in the north Adriatic where they are called mistral and bora respectively.

2 During the day high south-facing coasts see the sun and a seabreeze force develops.

This builds to a maximum tendency for on-shore winds (S) by early afternoon. With an opposing coastal slope effect (K) working against this there is a strange effect. There is a minimum of wind in the middle of the day when there should be a maximum if things were normal (page 24).

3 At such places the wind-speed graph is double-humped with a maximum of wind in the morning and another in the evening. Midnight sees least wind of all. Speeds are typical ones in knots. Note that these winds can arrive very suddenly and are confined, in their worst aspects, to the coastal regions. Strongest outflows occur when mountains top 2000–3000ft (500–1000m) and lie within 3 miles (5 km) of the coast. The wind slackens offshore.

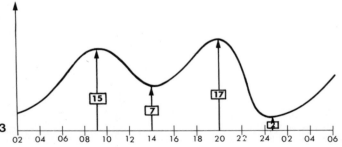

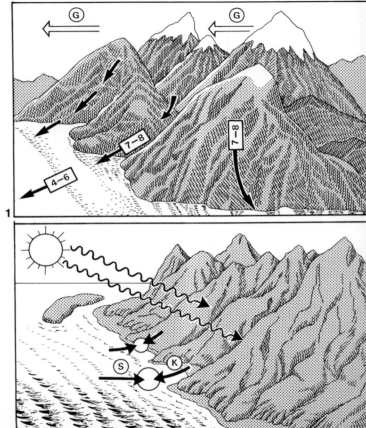

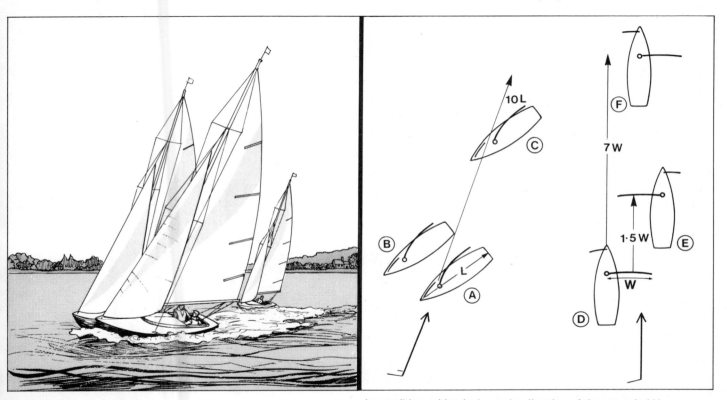

Blanketing Your Opponents
The cone of 'Dirty Wind' trails aft and to leeward.

Yacht (B) in the 'safe leeward position' will actually gain some advantage from being so close to A's sails. Yacht (C) in the 'impossible' position remains in 'dirty wind' up to ten boat's lengths from (A). The impossible position is down the direction of the true wind V_t.

Blanketing is most effective when the overtaking yacht (D) is about one and a half sail widths from the sail of the yacht ahead. Yacht (F) seven sail widths ahead of (D) would (in the absence of (E)) be just clear of blanketing.

51

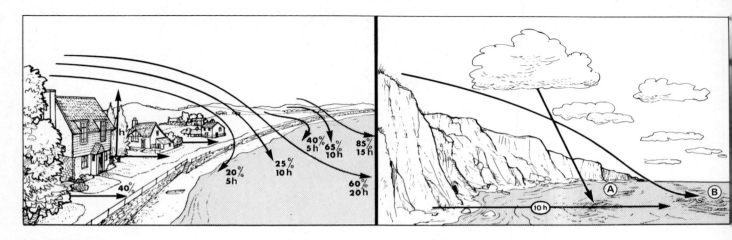

Wind Shadows

Barriers to the wind like groups or clumps of trees not only deflect the wind over them, but also filter the wind through them. The addition of the wind over to the wind through makes, for a moderately dense barrier (40–80 % covered), a situation where there is 40 % of full wind speed close in to the barrier, but this falls at 5h to half that figure. After this the wind climbs steadily but at 20h it still has only 60 % of its full speed. Open barriers show the same trend, but the speeds are higher.

A sea wall forms a continuous solid obstruction to the wind and, especially at low water, it shelters surprisingly large stretches of the waterways in its lee.

Solid barriers have zero wind in their immediate lee and then the wind climbs steadily being 40 % at 5h and 65 % at 10h. Yet a sea wall may be 20ft higher than the boat at low water so 5h is 100 ft (30 m) and 15h is 100 yds – well out or even across many creeks. When warehouses and boat sheds stretch along the waterway then the same rules apply – 40 % at 5h and nearly the whole wind speed at 15h.

Cliffs and Promontaries

The cliffy coast is a very solid barrier but when there are cumulus-type clouds about gusts come down onto the water at about 9–10h from the cliff top. This gust-edge at (B) will sometimes be made visible by more ruffled and therefore darker water there. When big Cu clouds ride over the normal gust shadow (A) then gusts can penetrate down closer to the cliffs. The zone (A) will have lighter wind, but it may be more turbulent than the zone beyond the gust edge (B).

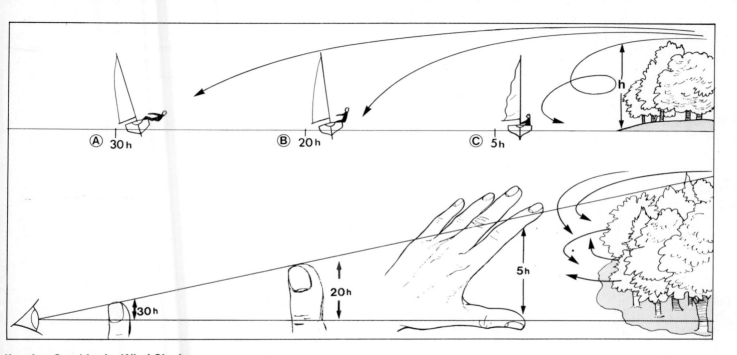

Keeping Outside the Wind Shadow

When the wind-hamper on the shore is trees and buildings that are not too dense, but not exactly sparse – and this applies to most venues – the zone to avoid is the 'zone of frustration' at 5 times the height (h) of the obstructions.

You can monitor this zone using your outstretched first finger and thumb held at arm's length. This yardstick will tell you when you are about 5h off. There is often more wind close under the bank in these conditions.

At 20h there will usually be about half the undisturbed wind speed and this distance can be monitored by the distance knuckle to tip of thumb held at arm's length.

You will be outside the wind shadow at 30h and your thumb nail at arm's length gives a yardstick for this distance off.

Allow for more wind closer in when it is a gusty day, but expect the chunks of increased wind to be interspersed with periods of very little wind.

Basic Lake Winds

1 Lakes are often long and narrow, and so, when there is a reasonable gradient wind, it will blow mainly along the lake either one way or the other. When conditions are quiet winds are generated as follows. East-facing slopes see the sun early and thermals occur there which induce anabatic winds A. A compensating flow occurs off the slopes still in shadow B. So wind ghosts to the sunlit side. Signs of these thermals are cumulus clouds.

2 In the evening the west-facing slopes see the last of the sun and there can be an anabatic drift onto them for a while so providing some evening zephyrs. Later, katabatics off both slopes lead to calm — and sometimes a backbone of cloud — along the middle. The latter occurs after dark.

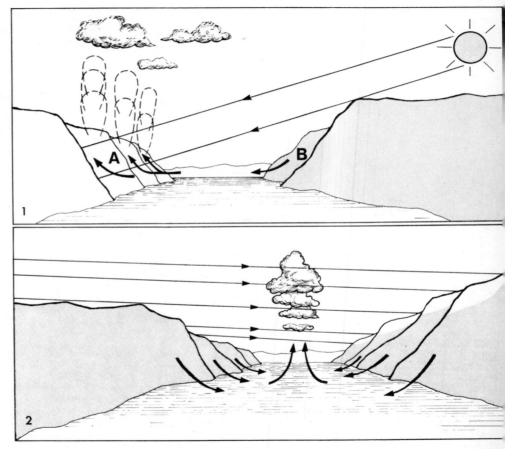

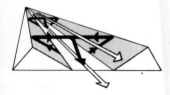

Mountain and Valley Winds

Sunrise. The mountain wind drains to the plains and anabatics occur up the slopes.

Early forenoon. The mountain wind falters and anabatics strengthen.

Early afternoon. The valley wind develops.

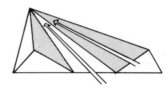

Late afternoon. Anabatics falter but the valley wind continues.

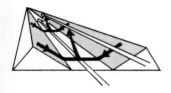

Evening. Katabatics set in and help feed the valley wind.

Early night. The valley wind falters but katabatics strengthen.

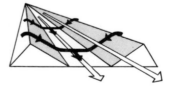

Middle of the night. Mountain wind begins to blow, aided by katabatics.

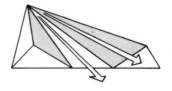

Early hours. Katabatics falter but mountain wind strengthens.
Based on a diagram in **Wind and Sailing Boats,** published by David & Charles, after F. Defant.

55

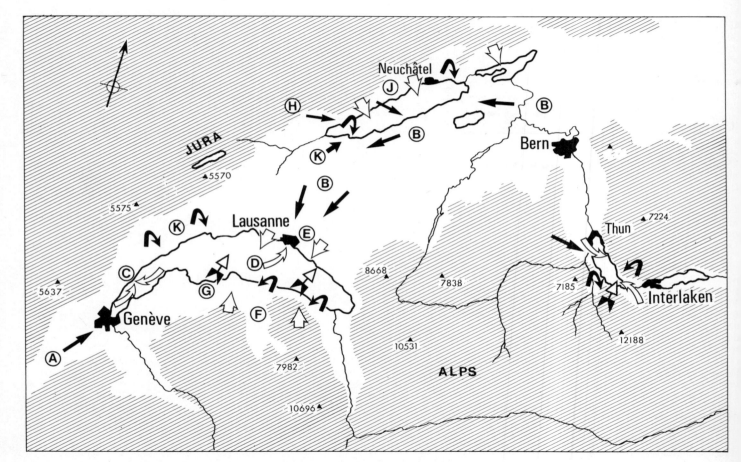

Actual Lake Winds

Lakes Geneva and Neuchâtel can be used as good examples of the kinds of winds that are actually found on inland lakes. The lake-plain lies between the Jura mountains to the west and the Savoie and Berner Alps to the east.

The Jura form a wall that stretches NE-SW not far from either lake and this will help canalise the local gradient winds either to come from SW or NE (sometimes N). La vent du sud-ouest (A) is entrained by the general southerlies ahead of depressions and so is a bad weather wind. The passage of such depressions brings in the Bise (B) and the winds flow along the plain more-or-less parallel to the mountains. Such canalised winds can grow to gale force.

The Sechard is the valley wind (p. 55) that blows towards the Rhône valley through the Petit-Lac (C) and the western part of the Haut-Lac (D) as a NE wind. In settled weather this valley wind will continue through the afternoon and evening. It is thermally induced and the sunshine that often precedes the developing southerly gradient winds of approaching depressions makes the two trends opposed. The resulting slight SW wind is called Vent Blanc possibly because of the appearance in the sky of cirrus and cirrostratus clouds.

The Haut-Lac develops 'sea' and 'land' breezes which will be weak and only the 'flat-lands' of the north shore around Lausanne are going to feel any sizeable effect. The lake-plain slopes from the Alps in the southwest towards Bern in the northeast. Thus valley winds will blow gently from SW hugging the ground in the early hours as well as blowing a few hundred feet up above the calm that exists at the surface. As soon as the sun can strike the slopes local to Lausanne it will create up-and-down currents and bring the wind to the surface so that a very light onshore breeze suddenly appears soon after daybreak on the Lausanne shore.

This early onshore tendency will be reinforced by a later 'seabreeze' effect, but the valley-wind is developing as a NE wind opposed to the breeze. The result is flat calm as the two effects nullify one another. The seabreeze effect is called Rebat (D) on this shore.

The nocturnal wind is strange. When the seabreeze effect weakens the valley wind develops as an off-shore wind along the Lausanne shore. It is called Morget (E) in the region of Morges. On the opposite shore a katabatic wind sinks off the Pre-Alps leading to another nocturnal wind called Chamoisine (F). The nocturnal winds can blow at up to Force 3 but the opposing tendencies yield strange winds and calms in the middle.

The föhn (G) arrives suddenly from over the Alps (p 58) and can blow at Force 6. Downdraught storms (thunderstorms) approach, from the Jura and the Savoie Alps. Violent and sudden gales can result.

The winds of Lake Geneva are not unique and similar effects appear on lakes throughout the world.

Consider the neighbouring Lac de Neuchatel that lies parallel to the Jura. The Bise affects this lake as it does Geneva and can rise to Force 8. The westerly winds (H) of depressions come over and fall down the Jura and may become Force 10. There is going to be a south-westerly when gradient winds are from the southern quadrants and the Jura steers them parallel to itself.

The katabatic that sinks off the Jura as the day wears on is called le Joran (J). It is unreliable but when the summits are snow-capped it can have mistral-type squalls.

Some winds have very odd behaviour that does not fit text-book ideas. When the gradient is developing for southerly winds they should be maximum in the afternoon. L'Uberre (K) persists in blowing in the evenings. The answer is that the valley wind effect is northerly and is also maximum in the afternoon. As soon as its effect slackens the southerly gradient wind can have its head.

Neuchâtel is closely under the mountains and downdraught storms will be sudden and forceful. The föhn may not reach here but lee descending winds replace it from over the Jura.

Föhn is more likely on the Thunersee as it lies closely under the Alps and is hemmed in by mountains. The mountain and valley wind system is classic here and reliable (p 55). In the forenoon the valley wind blows gently down towards Bern and after a change-over period blows up towards the Bernese Alps in the afternoon as a stronger Force 2–3 W to NW wind.

(More detailed notes on these winds can be found in 'Sailing on Continental Lakes' J. B. Moore)

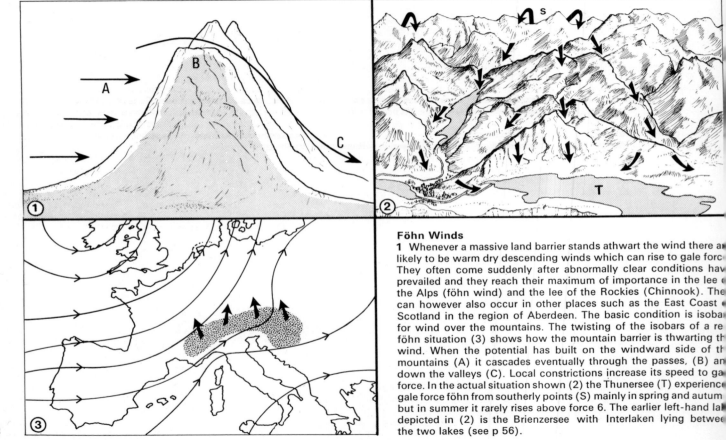

Föhn Winds

1 Whenever a massive land barrier stands athwart the wind there are likely to be warm dry descending winds which can rise to gale force. They often come suddenly after abnormally clear conditions have prevailed and they reach their maximum of importance in the lee of the Alps (föhn wind) and the lee of the Rockies (Chinnook). They can however also occur in other places such as the East Coast of Scotland in the region of Aberdeen. The basic condition is isobars for wind over the mountains. The twisting of the isobars of a real föhn situation (3) shows how the mountain barrier is thwarting the wind. When the potential has built on the windward side of the mountains (A) it cascades eventually through the passes, (B) and down the valleys (C). Local constrictions increase its speed to gale force. In the actual situation shown (2) the Thunersee (T) experiences gale force föhn from southerly points (S) mainly in spring and autumn but in summer it rarely rises above force 6. The earlier left-hand lake depicted in (2) is the Brienzersee with Interlaken lying between the two lakes (see p 56).

58

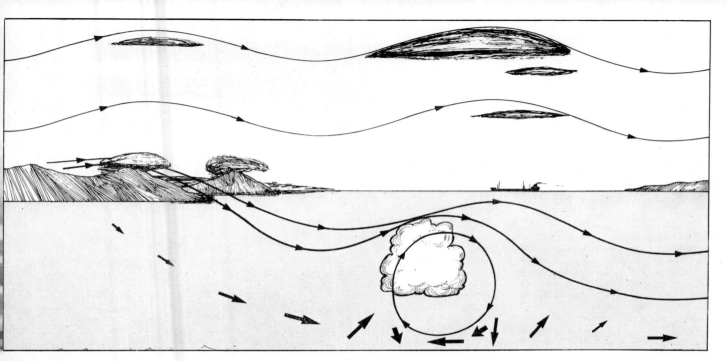

Wind in the Lee of Hills

Depending on the stability of the atmosphere and the wind speed different kinds of wind effects can be induced in the region up to 20 miles (30 km) downwind from a hill ridge. A quite modest but extensive hill ridge stretched athwart the wind sometimes induces waves in the airstream. That the conditions may exist is evident from sight of a cloud-cap (helm bar) over the ridge and lens-shaped clouds in their lee. The latter form over the waves and show where the most curious wind variations may be found. Directions may be widely different at any one moment within very short distances, but the conditions do not remain in one place. They move and so transport the wind variations with them. The only useful comment is sail towards or away from the hill ridge and hope to find more congenial conditions. It is worth noting that when under a lens-shaped cloud it loses its characteristic shape and appears dark and fuzzy — not light and smooth as when viewed from some way away. Cumulus airstreams are unlikely to show these effects.

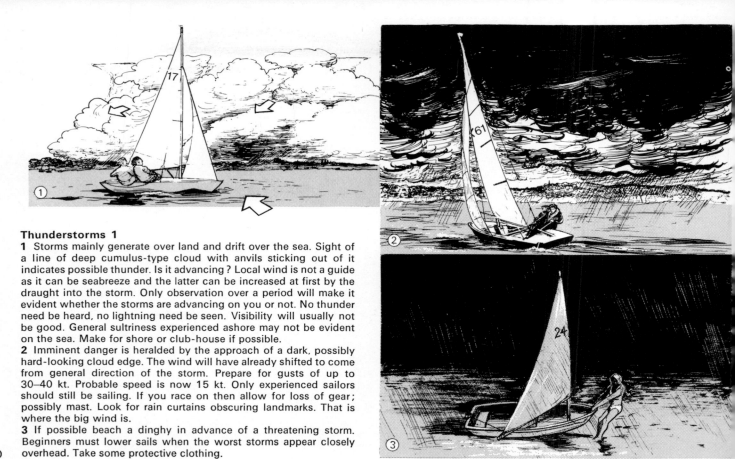

Thunderstorms 1

1 Storms mainly generate over land and drift over the sea. Sight of a line of deep cumulus-type cloud with anvils sticking out of it indicates possible thunder. Is it advancing? Local wind is not a guide as it can be seabreeze and the latter can be increased at first by the draught into the storm. Only observation over a period will make it evident whether the storms are advancing on you or not. No thunder need be heard, no lightning need be seen. Visibility will usually not be good. General sultriness experienced ashore may not be evident on the sea. Make for shore or club-house if possible.

2 Imminent danger is heralded by the approach of a dark, possibly hard-looking cloud edge. The wind will have already shifted to come from general direction of the storm. Prepare for gusts of up to 30–40 kt. Probable speed is now 15 kt. Only experienced sailors should still be sailing. If you race on then allow for loss of gear; possibly mast. Look for rain curtains obscuring landmarks. That is where the big wind is.

3 If possible beach a dinghy in advance of a threatening storm. Beginners must lower sails when the worst storms appear closely overhead. Take some protective clothing.

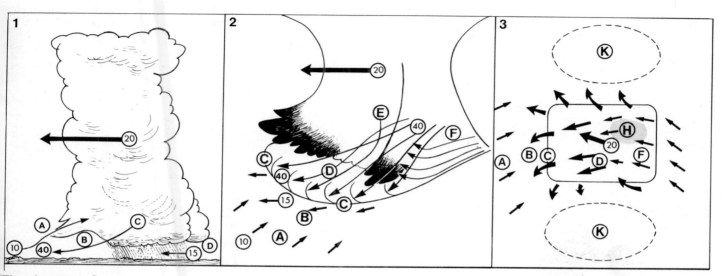

Thunderstorms 2

1 Bad storms come up against a wind that they generate themselves (A). Typical speed is 10 kt and the air lifts into an arch-cloud that hangs darkly over the 'nose' of cold air that is driving out from the storm (B), but the cloud may lift and lighten after the arch-cloud has passed. The impulsion for the thunderstorm wind comes from the downdraught (C) where the rain and hail are falling. The whole storm may only be travelling at 20 kt and can be 15 miles (25 km) across. In the rear of the storm (D) rain falls gently and winds lighten to a typical 15 kt.

2 The wind structure under an actual storm is complex. The wind flow is towards, but across the storm at (A). It shifts sharply or in a series of shifts at (B) to a direction from the storm. Typical speed 15 kt. When the cold-air nose arrives (C) sharp wind increase to 30–45 kt. Time this squall by the arrival overhead of arch-cloud that suddenly darkens the sea.

Some streamlines (D) come from rear of storm at the surface. Others (E) feed in from the downdraught or come in from the rear of the storm at height to dive down into the cold nose. Some (F) track in to lift over the (D) lines.

3 The typical ground plan of the winds under and around a storm is shown and the letters refer to (2). However (H) is where heavy hail is most likely and (K) is where daughter storms are most likely to breed. One storm cell may only last half an hour but its daughters take over and grow into storms that continue to breed until their fuel supply of warm moist air is used up.

may be intense. However winds do not often get above Force 6 except in some of the severe gusts that come with intense rain showers under high thunderstorms. Note that the whole thunder and lightning display may be a mile or more above the surface, whereas other storms are within 3000 ft (1000 m) of the deck.

1

2

Before the Storms

1 Storms in warm weather can grow at altitude along warm fronts. They are often preceded by special forms of cloud that foretell thunder. These specifically include lines of altocumulus clouds with small turret-heads like castle battlements growing out of them (altocumulus castellanus) and groups of small cloud elements that look like a flock of woolly sheep (altocumulus floccus). The day is often warm and visibility not good. There are curious sudden stabs of wind that produce a heel and then the wind may fall to almost nothing. It is often not above 10 kt mean speed.

2 Later, after the cloud of (1) has passed, the sky darkens and may look like this. The wind freshens but may still be odd in its gusts and lulls. Thunder will not break out yet but when it does lightening

Big Thunderstorms Inland

Sometimes on the sultriest days of summer storm areas of vast extent form with thunderstorms breaking out over hundreds of square miles. These storm areas form where the pressure is locally low inland and so they grow in the heat depression that always tends to develop over land in summer.

When a storm area is within striking distance of a coastline expect the following:

Seabreezes blowing in the early afternoon. These will help feed the storms that develop and may locally be intensified by them into a moderate or even fresh on-shore wind. Seabreezes clear the coast of cloud and may make storms seem unlikely. The radio may warn of trouble with news bulletins motoring flashes, reports of sports meetings etc.

A cold outflow of downdraught air is pouring out of the storm area and driving coastwards (C). Where seabreeze meets this cold outflow a sort of front forms with the seabreeze air lifted over the thunderstorm air blowing from inland.

iii The 'front (C) will move coastwards with the late afternoon and evening. It may move at 20 kt and so if storms are 40 miles inland expect the thunderstorm wind to blow away the seabreeze over the coast a couple of hours after the storms erupt.

iv The times shown are for the storms to break out and the wind to reach the coast but once started the storm wind may continue to blow for the rest of the night.

If storms are more than ten miles away then do not expect to be warned by hearing thunder or seeing lightning. The cloud mass may just be visible but visibility is poor on these thunderstorm days so the first you may know of the thunderstorm wind is when it hits you.

63

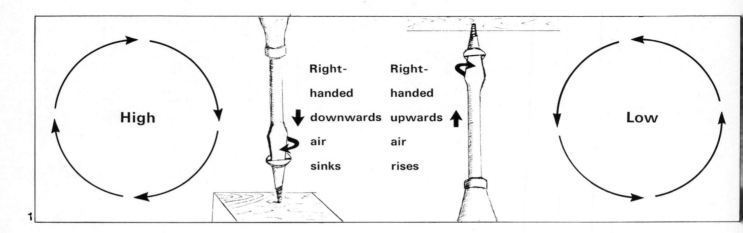

High

Right-
handed
downwards
air
sinks

Right-
handed
upwards
air
rises

Low

Looking at Weather Maps

1 The way winds rotate round centres of high and low pressure in the Northern Hemisphere (reverse for Southern Hemisphere) follows the rules for screwing in screws which are right-handed. Screw a screw downwards :- the sense of rotation is the same as round a High and shows the way the air sinks as well. The reverse is true for the winds round Lows.

2 (C) is cyclonic curvature of the isobars. The isobars bend to enclose low pressure. Here the weather is at its poorest for the conditions i.e. there is most cloud. Clouds that might not otherwise rain are induced to do so, showers are at maximum intensity etc.

(A) is anticyclonic curvature. The isobars bend to enclose high pressure. Here the weather is at its best for the conditions. Clouds will tend to disperse, rain will be light, showers will be small and tend to die out anyway. Fair weather predominates. Winds at night will be muted over and near land.

(S) is straight isobars. Here weather will tend to be between the two extremes, not very bad and not very good.

3 Where isobars wriggle locate the sharp or blunt vee-shaped portions. If these point away from High towards Low then they denote a trough which is a pressure 'valley'. So remember vees towards high mean a valley. These 'valleys' are troughs (T) where there will be more cloud, more showers, possibly rain, local squalls and thunderstorms. They may be frontal troughs (F) where all the above things occur but are enhanced. From a wind point of view the trough is not necessarily going to have a higher overall wind speed. In fact it may have a lower wind speed when the isobars curve most strongly. What is likely is that wind from aloft will be cascaded down by showers, thunderstorms and rain onto the sea surface and locally produce squalls.

Using the mnemonic above means that the ridges (R) are easily picked out as opposite to the troughs. Here skies clear, showers die out, rain if it occurs at all is usually from not yet dispersed frontal cloud.

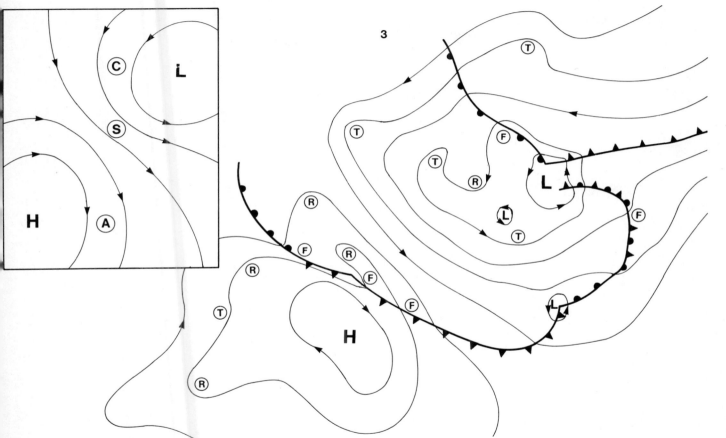

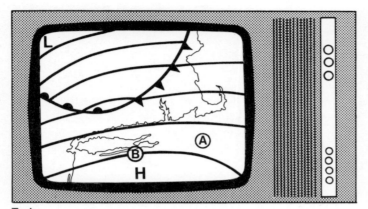

Today

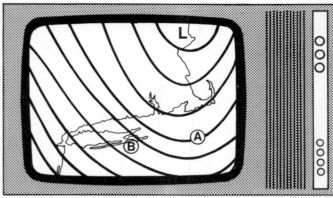

Tomorrow

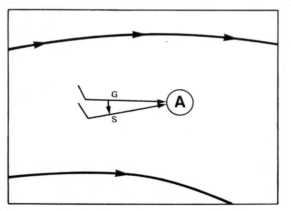

A Glimpse of the TV Chart

When you only catch a glimpse of the TV chart concentrate on your own area. For example on the east coast at (A) isobars are shown somewhat closer tomorrow so more wind than today. Isobars are curved anticyclonically today. Tomorrow they are likely to be cyclonic. Thus the extra wind will look and feel worse under grey skies. There could be showers in the trough especially in the afternoon. Wind direction aloft is along the isobars and is the gradient wind (G) (diagram left). To find surface wind (S) rotate backwards i.e. left-handed, through a small angle. Make it about 10–15° over the sea and anything from 20°–40° over the land. So wind today is SW and tomorrow will probably be SW to NW depending on how the trough moves.

Winds on today's tracks bring fair weather to (A) and (B). Tomorrow both are liable to showers and possible squalls as the main run of wind is from NW.

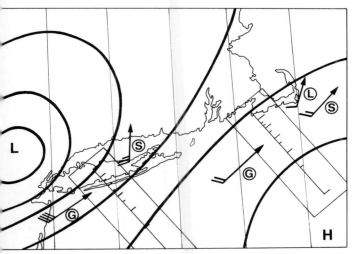

How Forecasters Forecast Wind

It can help to know how the forecasters arrive at the winds they forecast. First they have to produce a forecast chart with isobars that are as correctly spaced as possible. This is achieved by relating a surface weather chart (say for midday) to charts of winds in the upper atmosphere (contour charts) for the same time. Then using certain techniques the upper air charts are extrapolated forwards to the forecast time and the surface charts are also extrapolated for that time. The two are then married together and any inconsistencies ironed out. When surface and upper air forecasters are satisfied then the new surface chart will show where the Lows and Highs are most likely to have moved to by the end of the forecast period and the isobars between them can be adjusted to make them flow correctly.

The wind speed is measured from the isobars using a special scale called a 'geostrophic scale' because it is based on the apparent centrifugal force that provides the effect seen on p 27 and which is called geostropohic force. The geostrophic wind equation is complicated and so the forecaster uses a transparent geostrophic scale. He can then measure the speed and direction of the wind to be expected over any area. That wind is clear of surface friction and so he takes two thirds of it for wind speed over the open sea and one third over the land. He also makes allowances for places where the isobars are strongly curved, for there the wind he forecasts will not be correct.

The result is a forecast of the mean wind speed. The top of the gusts can be up to geostrophic speeds when they come down from several thousand feet up.

The wind only blows along the isobars at geostrophic levels (about 2000 ft or 600 m) and has to be canted in towards low pressure at the surface. Thus at (1) the geostrophic wind (G) is 40 kt SW, but at (S) the surface wind is reduced to 25 kt from nearer south. At (2), where the isobars are further apart, (G) is 20 kt and the surface wind over the sea (S) is likely to be 15 kt SSW while over the rougher land the surface wind (L) is only 10 kt or less and more nearly south. Where isobars diverge you cannot use a geostrophic scale. This is where 'light-variable' enters the forecast.

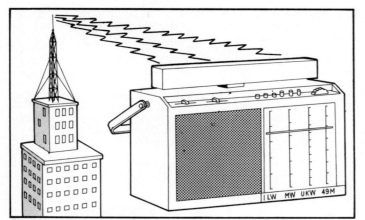

1

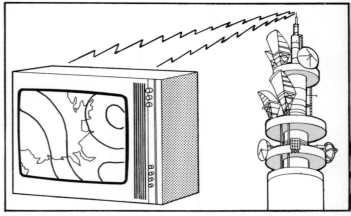

Weather Forecasts 1

1 and 2 Weather bulletins on TV and radio are provided by Are[a] Forecast Centres and are up-dated every six hours. They usually cover [a] state but in some case may cover only part of a state. These bulletin[s] look at the general weather conditions for the area for the period o[f] from 36 to 48 hours ahead.

Severe weather warnings are given headline attention in the bulletin[s] and are given when say severe thunderstorms with or without tornado[s] are expected or when severe squalls are likely to occur.

Otherwise the forecasts include expected cloudiness, whether it wi[ll] rain or be showery etc., what temperatures are expected, the wind spee[d] and direction and the humidity. The media will re-hash this material fo[r] their own purposes but the basic information is the same for all.

The five-day forecasts issued on Monday, Wednesday and Frida[y] can help in pre-race planning but the further ahead a forecast is mad[e] the less reliance that can be placed upon it.

3 In addition weather forecasts can be obtained by telephone an[d] details will appear in telephone directories.

3

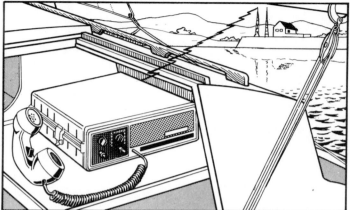

5

Weather Forecasts 2

4 If you require further and more personal information then the Area Forecast Centres will supply it by phone.

5 Marine forecasts and warnings cover weather elements essential for safety at sea. They include gale winds, especially when the latter are likely to shift suddenly; the incidence of heavy seas, the possibility of fog, heavy rain or snow which will seriously reduce visibility as well as ice hazards and freezing temperatures. Guidance forecasts for the high seas, coastal waters and the Great Lakes plus warnings of severe weather come from thirteen District Forecast Centres every six hours Local Weather Bureaux add to and localise these basic marine forecasts and broadcast them by radio to craft that have the equipment to receive them. Special forecasts are issued for all major harbors.

6 Weather charts can be seen on TV but are often better found in newspapers when careful study is required. Here will be found the forecast charts that are the Weather Bureaus considered opinion of what tomorrow's chart will look like.

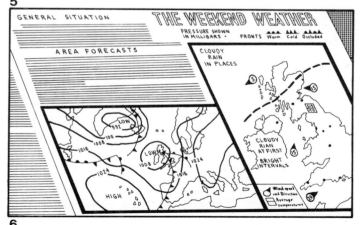

6

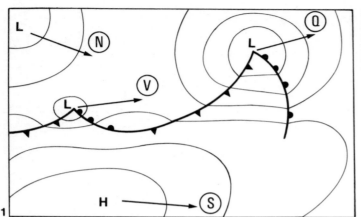

	rain	R r	
	drizzle	D d	/ = later
	snow	S s	So S 5–6/NW 6–7 = southerly Force 5–6
	shower	P p	at first becoming NW Force 6–7 later.
	hail	H h	Also
	thunderstorms	Th th	/W = later in the west etc.
	squall	Qq	
	mist	m	
	fog	f	
	haze	z	

Using the Forecasts 1 and 2

1 Gales blow up because pressure systems move, and deepen in the case of Lows or intensify in the case of Highs, or both together. The forecasts will use specific terms in describing the motion of centres.

The following terms are used to describe the speed of movement of Lows and Highs.

Slowly (S)   up to 15 kt
Steadily (N)   15–25 kt
Rather quickly (Q)   25–35 kt
Rapidly (R)   35–45 kt
Very rapidly (V)   over 45 kt

The kind of systems that move at these speeds are illustrated. Highs are sluggish and tend to move slowly (S). A Low in the prime of life will probably move rather quickly (Q). A wave depression will often move very rapidly (V) and deepen in the wake of the previous Low. A Low on the periphery of this system and destined to coalesce into a complex area of low pressure with the others may well move at normal speed (N) i.e. steadily.

A centre that is not moving anywhere in particular is described as quasi-stationary.

In taking down the shipping forecasts use can be made of the various prepared sheets sold by yacht chandlers. Useful abbreviations for present or past weather are shown. These are the Beaufort symbols and are internationally recognised. The use of the oblique stroke to represent passage of time cuts out a lot of words when attempting to follow the forecasts.

3 The weather forecast areas used in Marine Weather Reports refer to the areas shown here. Coastal reports are given for numbered areas of the Atlantic and Gulf Coasts up to 50 miles out. The deep-water areas are also numbered but in many cases carry names that make them more easily identifiable.

4 The areas for the Atlantic coast of Canada are named as in the diagram and overlap the US ones in the area of New England. Space precludes showing the areas for the Great Lakes and the Pacific coasts but these are easily obtainable.

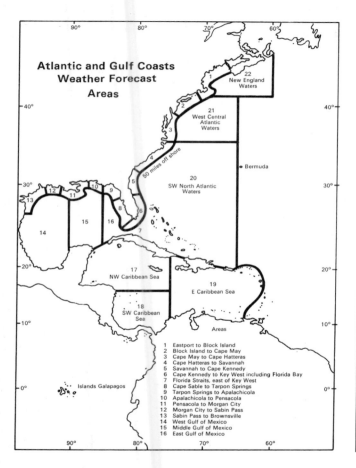

Atlantic and Gulf Coasts Weather Forecast Areas

1 Eastport to Block Island
22 New England Waters
21 West Central Atlantic Waters
20 SW North Atlantic Waters
50 miles off shore
Bermuda
17 NW Caribbean Sea
19 E Caribbean Sea
18 SW Caribbean Sea
14 West Gulf of Mexico
15 Middle Gulf of Mexico
16 East Gulf of Mexico
Islands Galapagos

Areas

1 Eastport to Block Island
2 Block Island to Cape May
3 Cape May to Cape Hatteras
4 Cape Hatteras to Savannah
5 Savannah to Cape Kennedy
6 Cape Kennedy to Key West including Florida Bay
7 Florida Straits, east of Key West
8 Cape Sable to Tarpon Springs
9 Tarpon Springs to Apalachicola
10 Apalachicola to Pensacola
11 Pensacola to Morgan City
12 Morgan City to Sabin Pass
13 Sabin Pass to Brownsville
14 West Gulf of Mexico
15 Middle Gulf of Mexico
16 East Gulf of Mexico

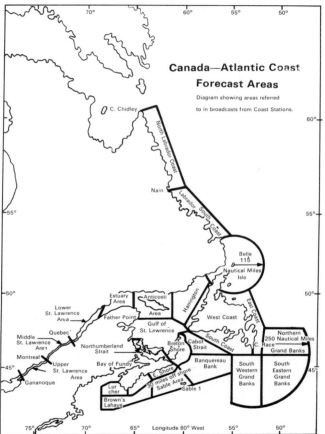

Canada—Atlantic Coast Forecast Areas

Diagram showing areas referred to in broadcasts from Coast Stations.

C. Chidley
North Labrador Coast
Nain
Labrador South Coast
Belle 115 Nautical Miles Isle
East Coast
Estuary Area
Lower St. Lawrence Area
Father Point
Anticosti Area
Harrington
West Coast
Middle St. Lawrence Area
Quebec
Gulf of St. Lawrence
South Coast
Northern 250 Nautical Miles Grand Banks
C. Race
Montreal
Northumberland Strait
Breton Shore
Cabot Strait
Upper St. Lawrence Area
Banquereau Bank
Gananoque
Bay of Fundy
E. Shore
30 miles off shore Sable Area
Sable 1
South Western Grand Banks
South Eastern Grand Banks
Lur cher
Brown's Lahave

Longitude 60° West

Land Area Forecasts			
	Beaufort force		**Knots**
Calm	0	○	0 – 1
Light	1 – 3		1 – 10
Moderate	4		11 – 16
Fresh	5		17 – 21
Strong	6 – 7		22 – 33
Gale	8		34+

1

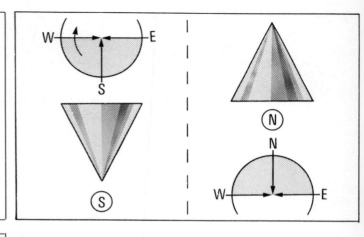

Gale = Force 8	**34-40 kt**	
or Gusts	**43-50 kt**	
Severe gale = Force 9	**41-47 kt**	
or Gusts	**52-60 kt**	
Storm = Force 10	**48-55 kt**	

Imminent = **0-6 hrs**
Soon = **6-12 hrs**
Later = **12 + hrs**

3

Wind Force and Gales

1 Land area forecasts use terms for wind speed that have specific meanings. These terms do not allow for the gusts so refer to p 22. Tomorrow's wind speed is difficult to forecast so take the forecast as a guide. If they say Force 5 then it is unlikely to be Force 2 but it might be Force 4 or Force 6.

The wind arrows fly with the wind and a long fleche can mean 10 knots or two Beaufort forces whichever is more convenient. A short fleche = 5 kt or one force.

2 Visual gale warnings are displayed at coastal stations and indicate that gale is expected or is present in an adjacent sea area. North Cone (N) is hoisted for gales from any point north of the E-W line. South cone (S) is for gales from any point south of the E-W line. Southerly gales are particularly likely to veer to NW or even N. From some stations (but very few) triangles of light in the same format are displayed at night.

3 This is a summary of the terms used to describe wind speed in gale warnings and also the terms used to indicate how long before the blow is expected.

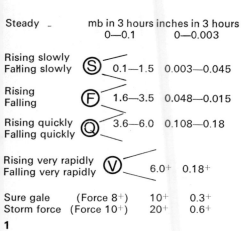

Steady	—	mb in 3 hours 0—0.1	inches in 3 hours 0—0.003
Rising slowly Falling slowly	**S**	0.1—1.5	0.003—0.045
Rising Falling	**F**	1.6—3.5	0.048—0.015
Rising quickly Falling quickly	**Q**	3.6—6.0	0.108—0.18
Rising very rapidly Falling very rapidly	**V**	6.0+	0.18+
Sure gale (Force 8+)		10+	0.3+
Storm force (Force 10+)		20+	0.6+

1

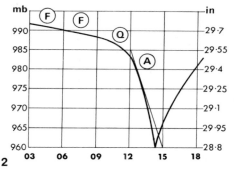

2

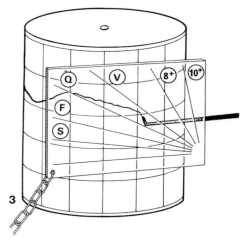

3

Barometric Tendency

1 Only the tendency of the barometer foretells wind not the actual height. The standard met. practice is given where tendency is assessed over a three-hour period. Appended are rules for the exceptional falls. If the tendency is 10 mb in three hours then Force 8 is normally inevitable. If greater than 20 mb then allow for force 10+.

2 The paper chart recorded by a barograph is a barogram. Part of a barogram where the wind rose to storm-force 10 or more shows that between 0300 and 0900 the barometer was falling (F), but this changed to falling quickly (Q). Then falling very rapidly and in this extreme event plunged to its lowest pressure at a rate which, had it been maintained for a full three hour period, would have dropped the barometer by a massive 45 mb. This is phenomenal and such gales only occur very locally and not very often (See *Heavy Weather Sailing*, K. Adlard Coles). To obtain the rate of fall i.e. number of mb or inches per three hours (standard met. practice) draw a tangent to the curve as at (A) to where it cuts a three hour period. At (A) the rate of fall is 25 mb/3 hr — enough to make it inevitable that a storm force wind will develop. The rapid rise after low is equally productive of wind.

3 For assessing rate of fall and subsequent gale force winds make a perspex scale with the rates drawn on it for your barograms. (S)=1.5 mb/3 hr. (F)=3.0 mb/3 hr. (Q)=5.0 mb/3 hr. (V)=7 mb/3 hr for normal rates of fall. For rises turn the scale over. For exceptional rates, mark (8+)=10 mb/hr and (10+)=20 mb/3 hr.

Falling very rapidly (V) is being assessed in the diagram. Force 6 probable and possibly Force 8.

73

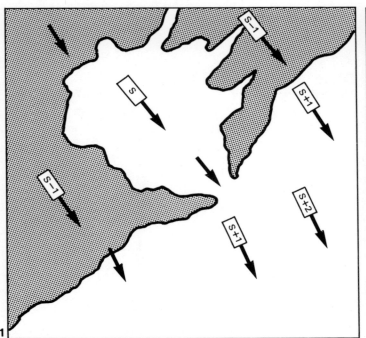

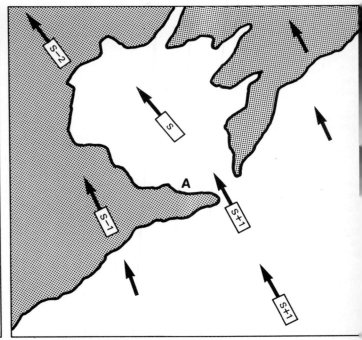

Wind Speed Ashore and Outside

1 The wind you feel in harbour is force S say. When wind blows from a general direction of land the wind ashore will be a Beaufort force less than S.

At sea, clear of the land or perhaps in the harbour entrance, it will be possibly two forces stronger than in harbour.

2 With wind blowing from the sea the wind in harbour is force S, but wi not be much stronger at sea, say S+1.

Where sheltered by the land it will be S—1. Example: tucked in th harbour at A the wind appears to be Force 4 (S—1). Wind at sea can b Force 6 (S+1).

Speed and Direction Ashore and at Sea

Under certain conditions the wind varies from place to place by amounts which are quite remarkable and we can illustrate this with an actual example. These winds were actually measured over northwest Wales.

(A) shows the calming effect that the land has on the wind. Force 5 on the coast falls to Force 2 after a short journey inland.

(B) shows the effect of a constriction where Force 4 over the promontary increases to Force 5 through the valley between the hills.

(C) shows the steering effect of mountains for W, Force 2 in the open steers into NW, Force 2 when thwarted by the slopes.

(D) shows how the wind is steered and slowed by steep slopes close to the sea and how even over an estuary the wind flow can be steered round through a right angle from its direction at sea when mountains lie in close proximity. The winds on the lake here are Force 3 from SW enhanced and steered by the mountains to windward and Force 2 from W along the valley.

(E) shows the way a narrow spur can split the wind into directions at right angles to one another on the two opposite sides.

(F) gives a perfect example of canalisation by a waterway for the wind at sea is Force 5 from W, but steers through the waterway first at Force 2 and further up at Force 1, but on the sheltered side there is calm (circled dot).

(G) continues the steering, but shows how the wind picks up speed and direction again across a wide bay.

(H) shows the effects of valleys and the very local directions and speeds that occur.

The diagram is based on an article appearing in *Yachts and Yachting* July 27 1973 and on an article 'Some Weather Patterns in Snowdonia' by D. E. Pedgley in *Weather* October 1971.

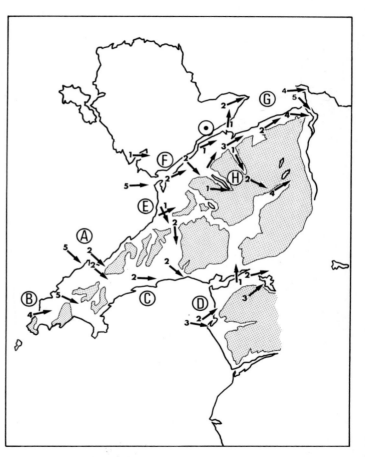

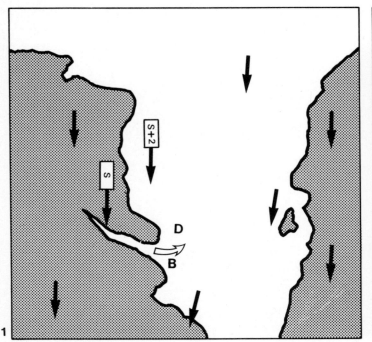

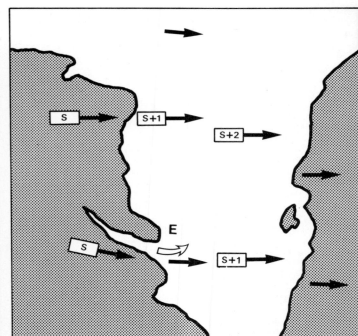

Shelter and Danger 1

1 In the extensive channelway depicted which is assumed to be 50–100 miles (80–160 km) wide the wind blows straight from the open sea and there is likely to be a heavy seaway near D especially if the tide runs against the wind. The wind can increase near B by funnelling.

2 The same channelway is sheltered by the land when the wind blows across it. This shelter extends well out to sea. The fetch of waves is short and so the seaway is slight near E except when the wind has blown for a long time from the same direction. On the leeward coast the seaway may be nasty for the wind is onshore with a long fetch and wave height grows with fetch. Coastal shallows along this coast should be avoided if possible.

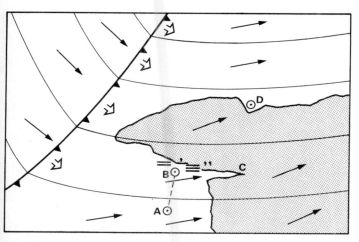

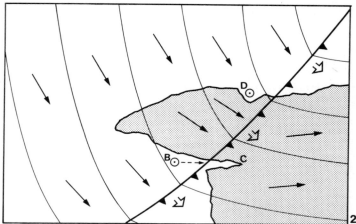

Shelter and Danger 2

Winds shift clockwise (veer) as fronts pass (Northern Hemisphere), so a coastal anchorage or haven that was sheltered can become exposed after a front has passed. Conversely a lee shore with a poor landfall can become a sheltered position with excellent visibility by a change of air mass as the front goes by.

There are examples of both around the lump of land depicted here. A yacht at A is broad-reaching for a coastal landfall in conditions of poor visibility (parallel lines=mist and triple ones=fog while commas= drizzle), but the situation will transform by the time he gets to B for the old front is moving down on him at perhaps 30 knots.

Situation **2** is 3 hours later. Now position B has gone from being a very nasty coast to being an excellent one, for the veer as the cold front passed now brings the wind over the promontary (assumed to be about 100 miles wide) and the cool clear polar air behind the front is in direct contrast to the misty tropical air conditions before.

Incidentally he also makes a fast time using the dictum
Sail towards the coming wind-shift
and is well set to enter the estuary at C.

A yacht at D, not much liking the conditions, tucks into an apparently safe anchorage, but has not allowed for the fact that should a front be in the offing the wind will veer and so expose his haven. Which is what has happened in (2). The isobars in this instance can produce stronger wind behind the front than ahead (it does not always happen that way) and so make the conditions at D even more unfavourable.

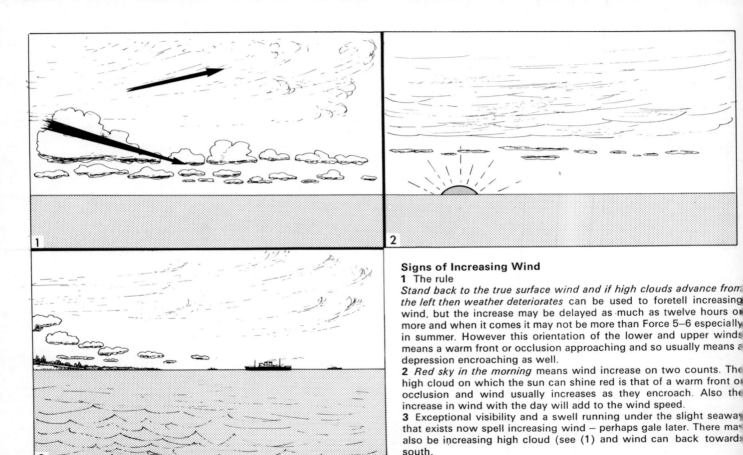

Signs of Increasing Wind

1 The rule

Stand back to the true surface wind and if high clouds advance from the left then weather deteriorates can be used to foretell increasing wind, but the increase may be delayed as much as twelve hours or more and when it comes it may not be more than Force 5–6 especially in summer. However this orientation of the lower and upper winds means a warm front or occlusion approaching and so usually means a depression encroaching as well.

2 *Red sky in the morning* means wind increase on two counts. The high cloud on which the sun can shine red is that of a warm front or occlusion and wind usually increases as they encroach. Also the increase in wind with the day will add to the wind speed.

3 Exceptional visibility and a swell running under the slight seaway that exists now spell increasing wind – perhaps gale later. There may also be increasing high cloud (see (1) and wind can back towards south.

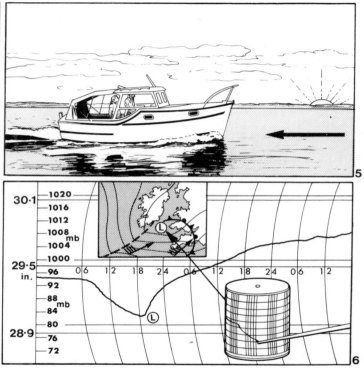

Signs of Increasing Wind

4 Winds tend to sink light in the evenings near land. The nocturnal wind will act against any tendency for on-shore winds and so if wind begins to increase from seaward when the sun is sinking, or has recently set this wind is being pushed against all the local forces and must be a pretty insistent gradient wind which could well grow during the night.

5 Dawn is a time when many people leave the shelter of harbour for the outside. It is also the time when the wind should be at its lowest speed. Wind that picks up from any quarter at dawn and shows any sign of increasing should make one suspicious that it may be lumpy outside later. Listen to a forecast.

6 In gale conditions after the weather has deteriorated to its worst point (L) there may be a respite while the barometer steadies or begins to rise. That rise must be interpreted as meaning that the respite is due to being in the centre of the depression and that a stronger wind from another quarter will soon strike. 'First rise after low foretells a stronger blow'.

This was the case in this actual situation which occurred during the 1957 Fastnet race and is covered in Adlard Coles *Heavy Weather Sailing*.

Winds and Fog

1 Sea fog is most likely when warm winds blow up from warm southern seas. Fog forms when moist air arrives over a cooler sea surface. It often forms first over coasts. It is rare on a leeward coast (L). Open arrows denote warm air and solid ones show cool air.

2 Signs of likely fog include (i) poor visibility, (ii) sinking funnel smoke, (iii) layer-type clouds, (iv) sweating deckheads, (v) a muggy feel to the air, (vi) wind less than 10 kt (force 4). Immediate signs include the formation of fog or low cloud over neighbouring coasts.

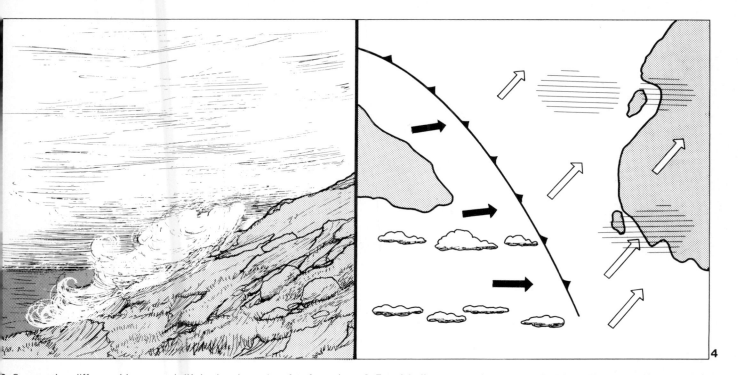

3 Sun on the cliffs provides enough lift in the air to clear fog from the immediate coastal belt. Later this may be helped by seabreezes or sometimes made worse when fog-banks off the coast are drawn in by the seabreeze. Occasionally there will be a clear lane close to a steep shore whereas to seaward it is thick fog.

4 Fog risk disappears when cooler air arrives. This often follows behind a cold front. Signs of a no fog-risk include (i) cumulus or cumulonimbus (shower) clouds, (ii) fresh feel to the air, (iii) rising funnel smoke.

Real wind=mean wind+gusts and lulls+turbulence

What makes the Real Wind?

(a) The real wind has an average direction and speed. This is the 'mean wind' (M), but for sailing boats the real wind is always gusting above and lulling below the mean speed and backing and veering about the mean direction. There are winds which spend very little time around the mean direction and these are often abnormally variable (page 91). For most of the time you will have a good idea of the mean wind direction and speed and you will know it more exactly at sea than near the land.
(b) The mean wind is a reference to which must be added the gusts and lulls and the backing and veering shifts. Such shifts are most in evidence over and near land. The wind shifts direction for periods measured in minutes and such shifts are 'tactical' in that you can use them to make extra way to windward etc. The wind usually shifts direction when it

changes its speed and the result is a 'real' wind which is always altering its direction and speed and to which a well-helmed craft must respond. The most usual state of affairs is that the wind shifts clockwise (veers) as it gusts (G) and correspondingly backs as it lulls (L).
(c) Surface features induce eddies (E) into the wind and these small eddies add to the variability of the pattern of veers and backs. They are not normally tactical in that they only last for seconds at the most. You cannot tack to such short-period shifts and they are a nuisance in that they tend to cloak the truly tactical shifts mentioned in (b). Turbulence of some kind exists in all airstreams. Gusts and lulls are due to convection currents and are most likely in airstreams with lumpy cumulus clouds.

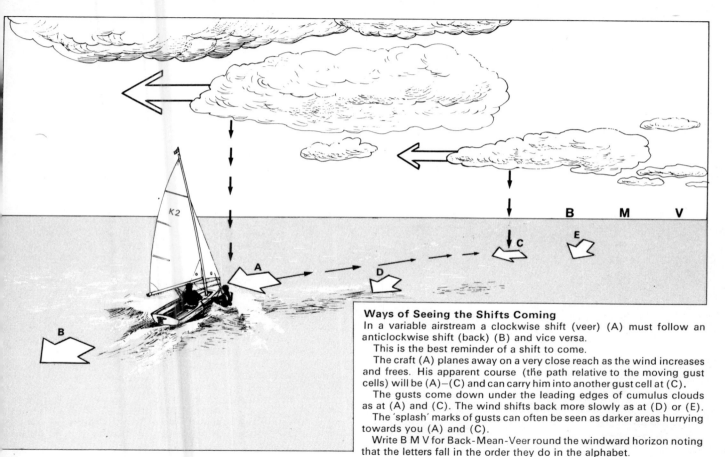

Ways of Seeing the Shifts Coming

In a variable airstream a clockwise shift (veer) (A) must follow an anticlockwise shift (back) (B) and vice versa.

This is the best reminder of a shift to come.

The craft (A) planes away on a very close reach as the wind increases and frees. His apparent course (the path relative to the moving gust cells) will be (A)–(C) and can carry him into another gust cell at (C).

The gusts come down under the leading edges of cumulus clouds as at (A) and (C). The wind shifts back more slowly as at (D) or (E).

The 'splash' marks of gusts can often be seen as darker areas hurrying towards you (A) and (C).

Write B M V for Back-Mean-Veer round the windward horizon noting that the letters fall in the order they do in the alphabet.

First Tactical Rule in a Variable Wind

1 The wind at the moment is from (A) and in making way to windward if it should shift more from the beam (from the land in this case) make up into it. However if it shifts more ahead (B) and continues to head you then tack (C).

Do not tack immediately in case it is just a heading shift from turbulent eddy which will pass in seconds. Hold on for as long as the count of 20 if needs be and if the heading shift persists then tack.

Tack on Headers

2 In a variable wind think of the coming shifts. From the helmsman's viewpoint on starboard tack the wind at the moment is (D) and he is making for the mark. The wind (D) is already shifted (veered) to his advantage so he does not think of tacking. Remember the turbulent shifts that you respond to by an undulating course, but do not panic into tacking to them. The next major shift cannot be seen but it must either be

   i) a veering shift that will make more way towards the mark, or

   ii) a backing shift that will force you to bear away from the mark.

In this example (E) is a veering shift and so the starboard tack boat makes up into it. However the wind has shifted so far that unless it is a permanent shift the wind must back (F) and head the craft soon. If you are waiting for such a shift (although you cannot be exactly when it will arrive) you can immediately respond to it by tacking.

3 The port-tack craft has a different wind (K) that is backed at the moment and therefore the helmsman envisages that the next shift must be a veer. This will head him on port tack and so when it arrives (L) he is prepared to tack thereby saving precious seconds.

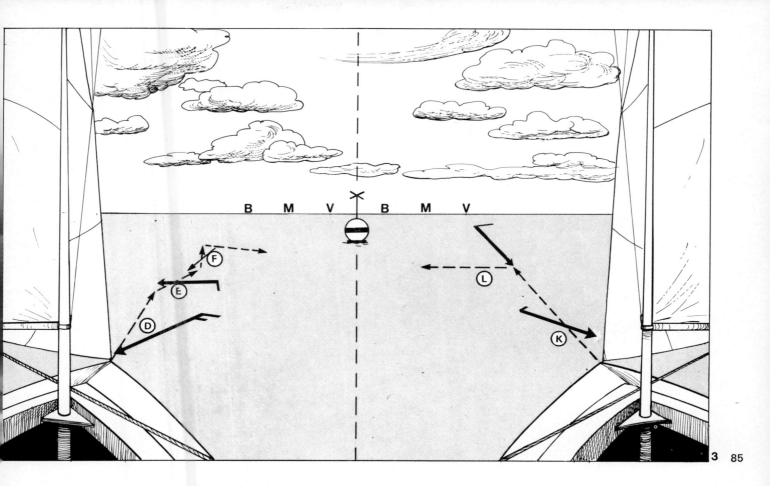

B M V B M V

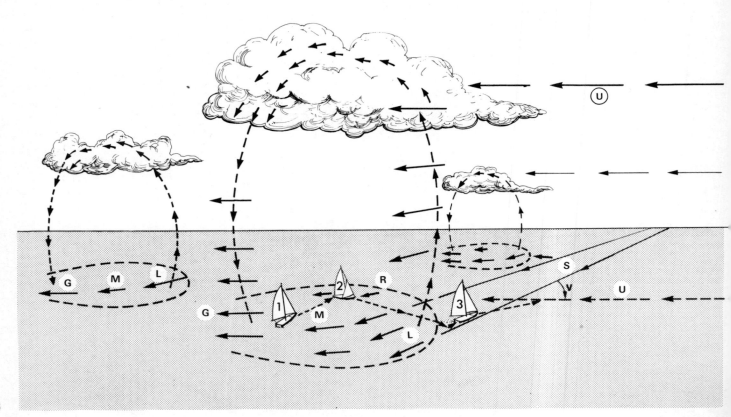

Gusts Cells

Most cumulus clouds are visible evidence of a wind shift pattern under them. What will happen to the wind direction and speed can be understood from the idea of a gust-cell — the region within the horseshoe-shaped dashed lines. At the head of a gust cell the air is fast moving having been brought down on a sort of conveyor belt from the cloud above. It has the upper (U) wind direction which is veered V to the surface direction (S). This is one of the gusts (G) that you meet sailing in this kind of cumulus airstream.

The dynamics of the gust-cell include a more-or-less complete circulation. The veer comes down under the leading edge of the cloud (that is how to recognise where the gust is to be found). This air from above is dragged by the friction of the surface so that it slows and shifts direction through the mean (M) speed and direction to where the wind is minimum. This is the lull (L) that has to follow the gust some time later. The lull air is warmed by the surface and rises back up towards the cloud so completing the circulation.

Gust cells may follow one another at regular intervals or they may have zones between them (R) where the wind shifts are more random. Look for the leading edge of the next cloud you are going to be under and so predict the next gust and veered shift.

The dinghy (1) is on the starboard tack to take advantage of the veer that the gust brings with it. Then as the wind shifts against him he tacks at (2) on to port to take advantage of the lift that he expects as the wind backs as it lulls in speed. Then at (3), having been forced to bear away at the gust-edge of the next cell, he has tacked back onto starboard. In this way he makes maximum way to windward.

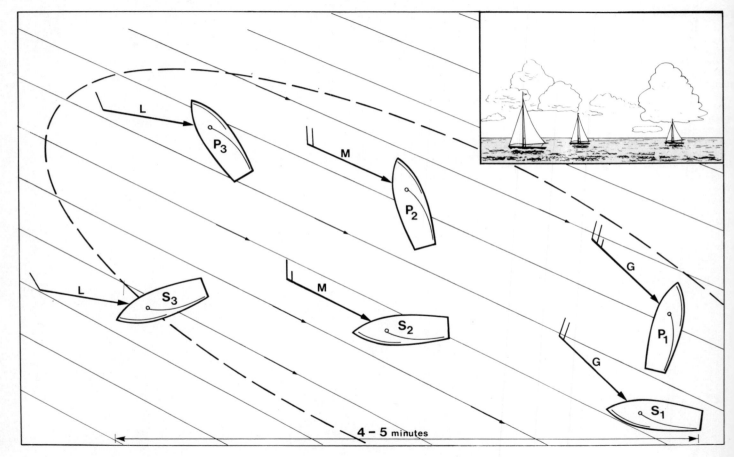

Tacking Through the Gust Cells

We find from studying real winds, that the wind usually tends to *Veer as it Gusts* and *Back as it Lulls*. When the wind variations follow this trend we call the airstream 'normal'.

There are many different shift patterns and the time between shifts is sometimes short and at other times long, but the usual time between one gust and veer and the next is about four minutes.

If you allow this to be a guide to the shift pattern on days with cumulus clouds you will see that a pattern of tacking to the shifts is perfectly possible. In fact 3–5 minutes is often all the time one spends on a given tack before some disturbance like another craft or the shallows or an anchored yacht dictates a tack. The exact moment of tacking may be more precisely dictated by the four-minute rule, in those airstreams that show it.

The other important refinement on 'tack on headers' that the four-minute rule provides is that the gust announces the veering shift that goes with it. And the following lull informs of the back that will accompany it. If you have a gust G then after a period of mean wind direction M you have to have a lull L – or else their could not be a mean wind. Thus the arrival of a gust says *'the wind should veer'*.

If the wind veers then maximum way to windward is made on starboard tack, S1. Whereas the port-tack yacht P1 must bear away in the veered wind. The tacks are neutral in the mean wind, but the starboard tack yacht S3 is forced to bear away as the wind backs in the lull whereas the port-tack yacht P3 can make up.

Thus we have a tactical rule in normal airstreams *Gusts – be on Starboard Lull – be on Port*.

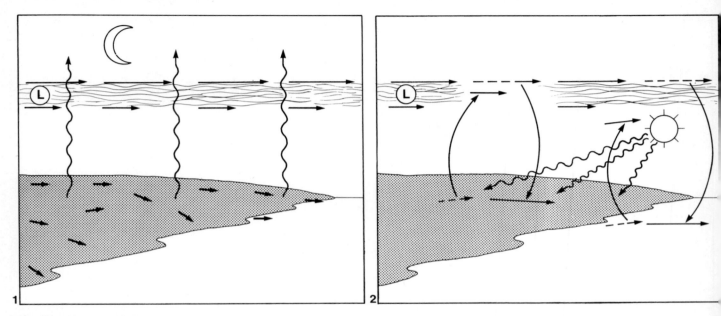

Inversions and the Wind

1 At night the land cools by radiation and the air below a certain layer (L) grows colder than that above. The layer (L) is an inversion layer (or simply an inversion). The wind below the inversion slows down by friction with the surface and the wind above it speeds up to compensate. Thus on any clear or partly cloudy night the surface wind goes down during the night – even to calm. Over the open sea this effect does not occur, but close to land the inversion effect spreads over coastal waters.

2 In the morning thermals break the inversion taking up slow night wind from the surface and bringing down faster wind from above the inversion. This speeds up the surface wind, but it comes in chunks at first and so the wind is often variable when the inversion is being broken. Soon there

are enough thermals to disperse the inversion altogether and then the morning wind is established.

3 On days when the surface air is already unusually warm the inversion is slow to break. Further – and very importantly – the wind above the inversion is strongly backed to the surface wind. Thus when thermals can bring down the wind from above the inversion it is strongly backed to the surface wind which is being lifted from the surface in the circulation of the thermals. Therefore as the wind increases it also backs strongly whereas the surface wind may sink to almost nothing at times. This pattern is opposite in its shift pattern to the normal pattern and so termed abnormal.

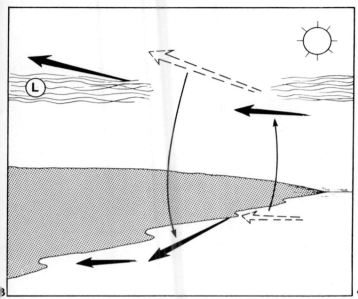

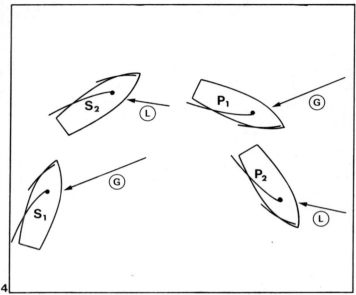

4 The tactical rule in an abnormal wind pattern is the opposite of that in a normal pattern. We can give a mnemonic L-A-S-T G-A-S-P

Lull in	Gust in
Abnormal	Abnormal
Starboard	Seek
Tack	Port

In abnormal patterns the gusts are fitful, but the shifts are wide especially in the mornings. A mean wind does not exist. The wind is either backed or veered or is going from one to the other. Starboard tack yacht S, is forced to bear away in the backed stronger wind (G), but can make up in the veered light wind (L). The reverse is true on port tack.

Sailing days 1 and 2   Cumulus Days

1 The events of the normal day when conditions are fair and cumulus clouds develop, but do not grow into showers are given in the sailing-day clock (left). For explanations of the normal and abnormal wind pattern see pages 88 and 91. The times are local sun time – GMT for Britain.

2 Seabreezes can only blow when the wind opposing them is less than 10 kt in the morning – in fact it should only be about 5 kt or less to make a breeze fairly certain. If wind blows on-shore then breeze aids the wind and fresh winds may occur in the afternoon. The sailing-day clock, for a seabreeze day when the wind in the morning is from the land and about 5 kt or so, shows that variations in the time before the breeze are most likely to be abnormal. Once the breeze sets in forget wind tactics.

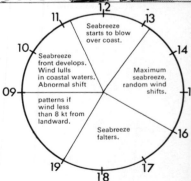

Left clock labels:
- Wind increases. Normal pattern develops.
- Maximum wind. Normal pattern.
- Cumulus develops. Wind picks up.
- Inversion forms. Wind and cloud decrease.

Right clock labels:
- Seabreeze starts to blow over coast.
- Maximum seabreeze, random wind shifts.
- Seabreeze front develops. Wind lulls in coastal waters. Abnormal shift
- patterns if wind less than 8 kt from landward.
- Seabreeze falters.

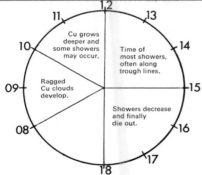

Sailing Days 3 and 4   Developing Showers

3 The sky from which showers develop is depicted in this drawing. The sailing-day clock gives the normal times at which the shower pattern takes on its various forms. (3) is a morning pattern, but it could also be a sky between groups or troughs of showers.
4 It is not normal for showers to occur at regular intervals (except possibly on coasts facing the wind). Relatively clear periods preceed and succeed groups of showers. These often come as troughs (depicted here). These troughs are most likely between mid-day and 3 p.m. Over the sea showers may go on day and night. Over the land they die out in the evening.

(clock diagram labels):
Cu grows deeper and some showers may occur.
Time of most showers, often along trough lines.
Ragged Cu clouds develop.
Showers decrease and finally die out.

Sailing Days 5 and 6   Over-warm days – Thundery and Fair

5 The warm humid kind of day with poor visibility and islands of thunder-looking clouds about very often comes from some easterly point. The wind is usually abnormally variable especially in the morning when the islands or flocks of quite high cloud will tend to disperse. This leaves a very warm middle of the day followed later by gathering cloud and probably thunderstorms.

Wind speed is usually below 15 knots but may increase to Force 6 when storms are brewing and gust to Force 8 or more when they strike.

6 The over-warm day for the time of year whenever it comes does no have to result in thunder. In fact several hot days usually succeed on another before the lower atmosphere develops thunderstorms.

The sky on these warm, but fair days often contain rafts of cirrocumulu or altocumulus cloud that are variable in time and place, but do no become extensive until perhaps late afternoon. Even than the cloud remains high. The light to moderate wind is usually abnormally variable (unless cumulus clouds develop in it).

8

...ing Days 7 and 8   Tropical Maritime Air

...hen the airstream is humid and from an oceanic region then it is
...ally very cloudy. There may not be much rain but the lumpy overcast
...persist for days. Stratocumulus in low layers which shows chinks of
...ter vein does not produce rain.

...he wind may be moderate or fresh and the cloud need not exist over
...sea, but develops as soon as the air gets a lift over the land. The wind
...ts but it can be very random in its backs and veers. It often clears
...denly or extensive breaks occur.

8 A moist oceanic airstream (tropical maritime air) may exhibit stratus.
This cloud covers coasts and hills and if the wind drops it becomes sea
fog. Its base may only be 100 ft (30 m) up at times and at its wettest it
produces flurries of drizzle. It takes time for such an airstream to 'dry out',
but it often does so via cumulus and stratocumulus clouds. The wind is
random in its variations.

Sailing Days 9 and 10   Coming Fronts – Old Fronts

9 A coming front. The sky ahead of a warm front or occlusion often looks like this. There is a layer of milky-white cloud up above with ragged cumulus clouds dying out below. The history should be one of fair weather gradually being invaded by high clouds, through the sky depicted here to darkening cloud layers and then a lowering cloudbase from which rain eventually falls.

The wind is often from a southerly point and quite variable but the variations do not fit the patterns on pages 86 and 91 except occasionally.

Expect increasing wind and listen for gale warnings.

10 Some fronts are old and do not even produce rain. Then all that r exist is a layer of dark stratocumulus cloud which is quite high and un it cumulus may develop. The wind here will usually be moderate or e light and the variations will be the normal ones we expect with cumu clouds, but the scale of the shifts is inhibited by the high cloud la preventing gusts being brought down from levels where the wind stronger.